UX for Developers

How to Integrate User-Centered Design Principles Into Your Day-to-Day Development Work

Westley Knight

Apress®

UX for Developers: How to Integrate User-Centered Design Principles Into Your Day-to-Day Development Work

Westley Knight
Northampton, UK

ISBN-13 (pbk): 978-1-4842-4226-1
https://doi.org/10.1007/978-1-4842-4227-8

ISBN-13 (electronic): 978-1-4842-4227-8

Library of Congress Control Number: 2018965466

Managing Director, Apress Media LLC: Welmoed Spahr
Acquisitions Editor: Jade Scard
Development Editor: James Markham
Coordinating Editor: Nancy Chen

Cover designed by eStudioCalamar

Cover image designed by Freepik (www.freepik.com)

Distributed to the book trade worldwide by Springer Science+Business Media New York, 233 Spring Street, 6th Floor, New York, NY 10013. Phone 1-800-SPRINGER, fax (201) 348-4505, e-mail orders-ny@springer-sbm.com, or visit www.springeronline.com. Apress Media, LLC is a California LLC and the sole member (owner) is Springer Science + Business Media Finance Inc (SSBM Finance Inc). SSBM Finance Inc is a **Delaware** corporation.

For information on translations, please e-mail rights@apress.com, or visit http://www.apress.com/rights-permissions.

Apress titles may be purchased in bulk for academic, corporate, or promotional use. eBook versions and licenses are also available for most titles. For more information, reference our Print and eBook Bulk Sales web page at http://www.apress.com/bulk-sales.

Any source code or other supplementary material referenced by the author in this book is available to readers on GitHub via the book's product page, located at www.apress.com/9781484242261. For more detailed information, please visit http://www.apress.com/source-code.

Printed on acid-free paper

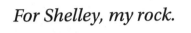

For Shelley, my rock.

Table of Contents

About the Author

 **Westley Knight** is a Web Developer turned User Experience Designer, husband to one and father to four, and now author living in Northampton, UK. He has worked in some capacity or another on the web since the turn of the millennium, having worked with small local businesses all the way through to large multinational corporations. He's worked for design agencies, in-house teams, and as an external consultant, and he has spoken at a number of conferences on how to embrace user experience design and its methods within your organizations and for yourselves.

About the Technical Reviewer

Ivana McConnell is the UI/UX designer at Customer.io, helping businesses talk like people. She loves designing intuitive experiences and services for digital and print. Currently based in Vancouver, she spends her free time rock climbing, running, cooking, and analyzing sports statistics. Find her on Twitter @IvanaMcConnell.

Acknowledgments

First and foremost, I wish to express my thanks to the team at Apress who have made this book possible, including Nancy Chen who was always there to chase me when needed, and to answer any and all questions; Jim Markham whose comments and editing have been very helpful indeed; and to all those behind the scenes who have made this happen.

Ivana McConnell deserves so much credit for the insightful comments and playing devil's advocate as the tech reviewer, and she has really helped to shape this book. A special mention must go to Louise Corrigan, whose innocuous message to me once upon a time sparked this whole thing into life. Last but not least, I would have never been able to finish what I had started without the continued support and positive thinking of my wife. Thank you, Shelley.

Introduction

From my first steps into professional website development back in October of 2000, up until the point at which I recognized that I wanted to build better digital products for people to use in May of 2010, I was largely oblivious to the user. Yes, it took me almost an entire decade to actually think about how other people may use the digital products that I was building. I would turn up to work and build what needed building, to the specification provided, for the client that was paying for the work to be done.

I don't think it was much of a coincidence that the revelation of "Responsive Web Design" was the catalyst that set me on my path to becoming a User Experience . Designer.

To be clear from the outset, this is not what I want for you as a developer, to completely embrace user experience foregoing all else, to change career and follow in my footsteps. No, my intention is to bring the disciplines of software development and user experience design closer together; to be able to work in such a collaborative way that the lines between the roles of the designer and the developer start to blur.

If, by the end of reading this book, you want to switch your focus and give in to that inner designer that is craving to get out, then good for you, and good for your users. But, if you only end up with just a little more awareness of the effect that the digital products you build has on the people that use them, well, that's the first step on your path to becoming a more user-centered developer.

CHAPTER 1

What Is User Experience?

Over the past few years, the prominence of the term "User Experience" has grown significantly. The term, coined by Don Norman, was not created to simply focus on digital products, but to encompass the entire experience that an individual has, through any and all mediums, around a product or a service.

This is the purest understanding of the term User Experience (UX), but as Don himself has said, the term has been "horribly misused" when it is applied specifically to the context of websites and applications alone. With that said, the core concept of UX endures; regardless of what kind of digital product the user interacts with – whether that be a website, an application, or any other piece of software – UX is still about the experience a person has with that product.

However, this book presents a slight variation of the concept. As the title suggests, it will focus on User Experience for Developers, in regard to how they can contribute to a better experience for the end user through the digital products they build (although this deviates from the original meaning of the term). As developers we have our own window through which we can affect the user experience. We find ourselves at the sharp end of the software development life cycle: at the point of implementation. We are turning the intentions of product owners, analysts, and designers into products that will be used by real people.

Creating an experience isn't about the how a product is created. It's not about how it was engineered, what frameworks were implemented, or whether you use bleeding-edge technology; it's about how the product helps people to complete their tasks, to achieve their goals, and – perhaps most importantly – how they feel when they use and engage with the product.

This user-centered mindset can be a commonly neglected aspect of digital product design, and is one that needs to receive far more prominence. By providing developers with the means to gain a comprehensive understanding of your user's needs, and what good user experience means to your users, we can create more successful digital products with a solid foundation of knowing their needs and goals.

© Westley Knight 2019
W. Knight, *UX for Developers*, https://doi.org/10.1007/978-1-4842-4227-8_1

1

Typically, the term User Experience refers to how an end user feels about the digital products that developers build, but you cannot design the experience itself; that belongs to the user, to the individual. Their experience is formed in their own mind, through a filter of their previous experiences, the situation they find themselves using the product in, and a multitude of other influencing factors. An experience is as unique as the individual that perceives it, which makes it a completely subjective matter. This means that we can only design for an experience, to aim to give the user the best experience we can by designing to meet the needs of the user, in the situational context they may find themselves in while they use the products we create.

The goal of this chapter is to understand what User Experience means to a developer building a digital product. This will be the context in which we continue to uncover the improvements we can make to our own understanding, our day-to-day workflows, with our project teams, with designers, with our fellow developers, and ultimately, the people who will be using what we build.

We'll look at how we can define what user experience is, firstly by working through what it is not; breaking down common misconceptions; differentiating the often-conflated user interface against user experience; and examining the various disciplines that come together to form the overarching user experience. We'll also examine where user experience fits in as part of a process, how it fits with the needs of your organizations, and how it fits with your own responsibilities as a developer.

Defining User Experience

User Experience is a notoriously difficult thing to define. Ever since I entered the field, I have been looking for the perfect answer to the question, "What do you do for a living?"

As a Front-End Developer, I could answer this question with relative ease to those who operate outside of our technically focused bubble: "I build websites." More often than not, this answer was fairly well understood, although it would lead to the occasional "Can you help me fix my email?" predicament.

Answering the same question with "I'm a User Experience Designer" leads to some of the most genuinely entertaining expressions I have seen appear on the faces of human beings. The ensuing awkward silence is then filled with my own rambling explanation of how I work to make applications or websites easier to use. This then leads to the design world equivalent of "Can you fix my email?," which is for the other person to pull their mobile phone from their pocket, and walk you through the most annoying thing to them in the app they use most at that moment in time.

After this happens to you a few times, you start to build an understanding of how everyone is affected in different ways, not only by the product they use, but also in the contexts they find themselves in, the tasks they are looking to complete, alongside a multitude of other factors that the team of people who created the product in the first place could never have imagined.

Misconceptions of UX Design

Whether or not there is a real understanding of what User Experience Design truly is across all industries and organizations is up for debate. In my experience, the vast majority of organizations that I have come into contact with are still coming to grips with User Experience, what it entails for their business, and figuring out how it changes the way they operate when trying to make the users – their customers – an integral part of the process when designing, building, or updating their digital product.

Although we have established that the term User Experience has been misused when compared to its original meaning, and even if we reframe UX to purely focus on digital products, there are still a few misconceptions around what comprises the user experience.

The most common of these misconceptions is that User Interface Design is seen as synonymous with User Experience Design. So let's take a look at setting a few things straight.

UX Is Not UI

As any UX practitioner will tell you, user interface design is not user experience design. UX practitioners will look to educate others that the scope of UX Design reaches far wider than just the discipline of UI Design, while looking to avoid diminishing its importance to the overall user experience.

Figure 1-1 shows the User Experience design disciplines, as envisioned by Dan Saffer.

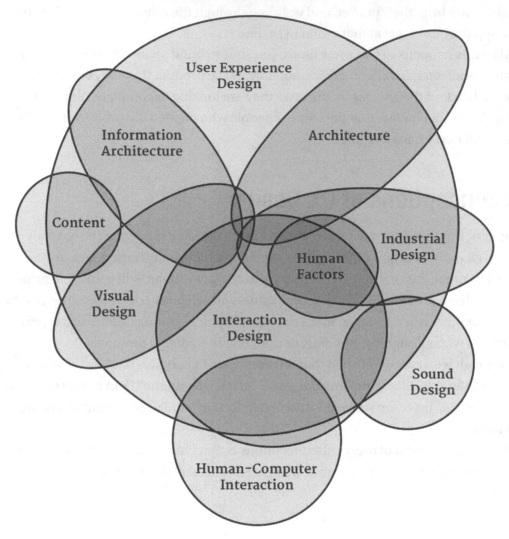

Figure 1-1. *The Disciplines of User Experience*

Although this is not an exhaustive list of all the facets that could be considered part of user experience design, from this you can see how User Interface Design sits within the larger sphere of Interaction Design, which in turn belongs to the sphere of User Experience Design.

Depending on the structure or strategy of the organization that you work in, each of these disciplines could be the responsibility of separate individuals. Perhaps each is a discipline shared between multiple people, or there may be one individual covering multiple, or perhaps even all of these disciplines.

If we think about these disciplines and how they relate to the roles of people within an organization, we may find that a team working on a particular feature of their flagship product would include a User Researcher who studies Human-Computer Interaction in relation to your product. A Content Strategist or Copywriter who would work on Content, and perhaps Information Architecture. They may have User Interface Designers who only work on Visual Design, or the same role may also cover Interaction Design and Sound Design. There may be a full team of individuals who specialize in each of these disciplines working together, or there may be a single individual who covers all aspects of User Experience Design: the fabled UX Unicorn.

Whatever the make-up of the team, and whatever disciplines fall into the responsibilities of a particular role, it is apparent that all of these disciplines – all of these aspects of user experience design – must be considered in order to deliver a better experience to the user.

"Design is not just what it looks like and feels like. Design is how it works."

—Steve Jobs

We must also be mindful not to restrict our understanding of the user experience to simply that of visual design, or the graphical user interface. We must expand our understanding to the physical connections we have to the products we are using; input through peripherals like the mouse and keyboard, direct physical interactions with touch screens or multi-touch track pads, and the physical responses we receive from those interactions through haptic and kinesthetic feedback. With voice interfaces becoming more common with Amazon's Alexa, Apple's Siri, Microsoft's Cortana, and Google Now, we must consider how users may wish to interact with our products in this way. With virtual reality making a seemingly promising resurgence, as well as augmented reality and gesture-based interactions, we find that a user's experience reaches far beyond the traditional graphical user interface, and that there are many more ways of interacting with our digital products than is immediately apparent.

UX Is Not Usability

It is common for usability to be thought of as the user experience, as the term is used to describe what a user thinks and feels about an interface; how intuitive it is, how easy it is to use, how easy it is to learn. Again, usability is just a small part of the larger user experience whole. When we examine what usability means – how easy it is to use and learn – it becomes apparent that it is an attribute of the user interface.

As usability applies to the user interface, again, this is not just related to the visual aspect, but to all mediums through which a user can interact with our digital products.

People often think that making a product usable creates a good user experience. As we have already established, there is more to it than that. While usability is most definitely an important factor that contributes to the user experience, only concentrating on usability neglects other aspects of the experience.

The UX Honeycomb in Figure 1-2 illustrates the other facets that we need to consider in a more holistic view of a user experience.

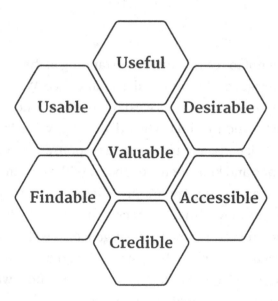

Figure 1-2. *UX Honeycomb created by Peter Morville*

The UX Honeycomb was created by Peter Morville to help his clients understand that there was more to the user experience than just usability. Each facet is representative of a part of the user experience:

- Useful – If your product does not solve a problem or fulfill a need that its user has, then the need for that product quickly evaporates. We must always be aware of our users and their changing needs and behaviors in order for our work to stay relevant and useful.

- Usable – Ease of use and learnability are key to retaining those who already use your product, and yet it only relates to the user interface. Although important, it does not encompass all of the considerations required for good user experience design.

- Desirable – Although this is rather intangible, the importance and value that elements of emotional connections to a brand, an identity, or a product can have significant bearing on the overall experience.

- Findable – A user must be able to find what it is they need to be able to get the job done.

- Accessible – We must strive to make the things we build available to everyone, regardless of physical or cognitive impairments.

- Credible – The product must be trustworthy. It must allow the user to believe what we tell them.

- Valuable – The product must deliver value, not only to the user's satisfaction, but to that of the stakeholders, and to the bottom line of the business.

UX Is Not Just Part of a Process

Something that I still encounter is that there can be a large divide between the user experience designers and the developers working on the same product or feature. This is especially surprising when the developers are employing Agile methodologies. The iterative and incremental nature of Agile development is so closely aligned to the process of user-centered design, it can be completely mystifying that the larger life cycle of a project still follows a more traditional waterfall process, where design work will be completed before handing documentation over to the development team for their work to begin. It really is more common than you may think.

User experience design is not an item on a list where you can check the box and say you're done. It is an essential part of every process, or in other words, it is the process. Placing the user at the heart of the design process requires the integration of user experience design into everything you and your team do.

From the very beginning of the software development life cycle for any given feature of a digital product, we should be looking to include the user. Their involvement will help to guide the decisions we make at every step of the journey from inception to launch, and beyond. User research can be utilized at the very beginning to validate ideas for features, whether they would be useful to the user in helping them to complete their tasks and achieve their goals. Prototyping and usability testing with real people help us to quickly iterate our proposed design into a more usable solution.

Our work involving the user is not finished when a feature is released to the world. Analytics and varying forms of user feedback can be utilized following the launch of a feature to feed back to the business to see how we can further improve our offering to our users.

A user's needs and behaviors are constantly evolving, so in order for your product to stay relevant to them, there must be a constant effort to respond to those needs. This means that the work you do, whatever it may be, is never truly finished.

UX Is Not Only About the User

Unfortunately, some of the terminology used to convey the meaning of a particular approach can be misleading in some cases. Take, for instance, the term "user-centered design." You could be forgiven if you were to draw the conclusion that the user was at the heart of every decision made in this approach to design.

As much as I would love this to be the case, as I'm sure many other UX practitioners would, this is simply not how the real world functions. User-centered design (also referred to as Human-Centered Design by IDEO, a global design company) actually refers to bringing the needs of the user into consideration from the very beginning of any project. The representation of user needs should ideally stand on an equal footing alongside both the business objectives and technical requirements (Figure 1-3).

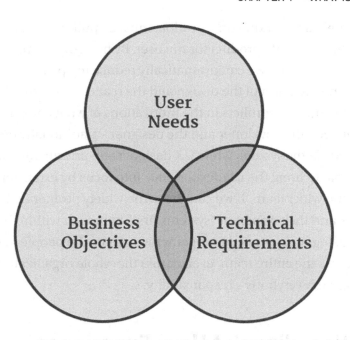

Figure 1-3. *Human-Centered Design adapted from IDEO, a global design company*

This also means that we cannot always do what is best for the users. In the real world, you will find many cases in which the business goals override the user needs. In this situation, we are aiming to meet as many goals and needs as is feasible in our best efforts to make the best possible product within the constraints we have.

UX Is Not the Responsibility of Someone Else

In the same vein that UX Design isn't just one stage in the larger process, it is part of everyone's process, whether they are aware of it or not. The user experience is affected with every decision made about the product, from a strategic business perspective, right down to how a button is implemented in the product itself.

In order for every role in the process of creating digital products to take on the responsibility of the resulting user experience, user-centered design must become part of the organizational culture. Everybody must be pulling in the same direction in order to build the best product for their users. If your organization isn't driven by user needs as much as they are by the business goals, together we can start to affect change by bringing the roles of the UX designer and the developer closer together.

Everybody in the team working on a product must be pulling in the same direction in order to build the best possible product for the user. By bringing the roles of UX designer and developer closer together, we can dramatically reduce the possible (and probable) disparity between the intention of the design and the realization of the product.

By removing the internal conflicts in the motivations of what constitutes a good digital product between the developer and the designer – traditionally developers are focused on the needs of the system, while UX designers on prioritizing the needs of the user – we are able to bring the user experience into focus by extension: not just for ourselves, but for the wider team. If we can break the widely proliferated stereotypes around developers and their apparent "systems first" approach within the team – specifically by focusing on user needs – together we can be the people to instigate the change needed across the entire team, even across the whole organization, making the user experience part of everybody's responsibility.

The Core Disciplines of User Experience

Since there are so many different interpretations of what user experience design comprises, it can be rather challenging to define the job roles that exist within. UX Design, as an industry, is still maturing, and we will continue to see this process of maturation throughout businesses across the world as the approach of user-centered design is assimilated into the day-to-day workings throughout the organization.

In my opinion, "The Six Core Disciplines of User Experience" defined by Nick Finck is the blueprint within which individual roles can be categorized. It takes the array of different disciplines found in "The Disciplines of User Experience" by Dan Saffer (Figure 1-1), and refines them into a set of specialties that focuses on the areas of endeavor most commonly found when creating digital products. Let's take a brief look at each of these core disciplines to see what they involve.

User Research

The focus of user research is to understand the needs and behaviors of your users through observation, task analysis, and other methods of gathering feedback in order to interpret the effect a design has on those users.

Content Strategy

The aim of content strategy is to ensure that your product is home to meaningful and engaging content. The discipline focuses on the planning, creation, delivery, and governance of content to deliver useful and usable content to the user.

Information Architecture

The aim of the discipline of Information Architecture is to help users to understand where they are, where they have been, and what to expect next, as they navigate through information in order to achieve their goals. Understanding how items of content relate to each other, and then organizing them in a logical, meaningful, and sustainable manner accomplishes this.

Interaction Design

Interaction design is the practice that looks to create meaningful and engaging interfaces by understanding how users interact with technology. It enables us to guide users through journeys by giving them clues about what the next steps are, make users more efficient by anticipating and mitigating possible errors, provide responses to a user's actions in the form of feedback, and ultimately make it simple for the user to learn the interface.

Visual Design

Good visual design enhances a user's experience and builds their trust in the brand by focusing on aesthetics. It aligns the typography, colors, images, and other visual elements to help convey the content or function of the product.

Usability Evaluation

Usability refers to the efficiency and effectiveness that a user experiences when interacting with a digital product. Different techniques can be implemented to determine how intuitive the design is, discover the frequency of errors when carrying out tasks, reveal how easy it is to learn and use, and even measure subjective feedback in terms of user satisfaction.

Summary

We have covered the definition of user experience in the context of digital products: websites, applications, or other software. By addressing common misconceptions of user experience and the discipline of user experience design, we have built a solid foundation of understanding that will stand us in good stead for the topics we will cover in the rest of the book. We'll look at how the perspective of the user should influence your day-to-day working practices, how we can more effectively work within our teams to deliver better experiences for our users, and the practical implementation of tools and techniques required to become a user-focused developer.

CHAPTER 2

The Importance of User Experience

Back in January of 2012, Jakob Nielsen published an article, "Usability 101: Introduction to Usability". In it, Nielsen states, "usability is a necessary condition for survival." If a user is unable to find what they're looking for, if they find the product difficult to use, or simply get lost in trying to achieve their goal, they will leave.

From the launch of the first iPhone back in 2007, there has been an explosion in terms of internet traffic coming from mobile devices. Statcounter reported that internet usage by mobile and tablet devices exceeded that from desktop devices for the first time in October 2016. In September 2016, Google released statistics that 53% of mobile sites are abandoned after 3 seconds.

With these kinds of figures in mind, it would be fair to extend Nielsen's statement on usability to say that a good user experience – or at the very least a better user experience than your competitors – is now a necessary condition for survival, and usability is now just one of the steps in creating successful digital products. These days, if two separate products exist that enable a user to complete the same goal, the one that is more enjoyable to use, the one that provides a better user experience, will be the one that succeeds.

As we noted in the previous chapter, user experience design requires us to bring the user into the heart of the design process. We should always be aiming to improve the lives of our users – however grand a statement you may feel that is – by making it easier for them to complete their tasks, achieve their goals, while also making it enjoyable for them to do so.

© Westley Knight 2019
W. Knight, *UX for Developers*, https://doi.org/10.1007/978-1-4842-4227-8_2

Beyond that, there must be an understanding that a good user experience cannot exist without underlying support from the business. With the continuous advancements of technology and the increased expectations of our users, there is a constantly increasing likelihood that if an organization doesn't consider the user experience they deliver to be of any importance, they won't last very long in this age of digital disruption.

UX from the Business Perspective

It's fair to say that over the past few years the term "User Experience" has become more and more prominent throughout those organizations that have some level of investment in digital. The "digital disruptors" of the world, without a doubt, have encouraged the rise of User Experience in the business world. These "digital disruptors" are those digitally centered organizations that leverage advances in technology and the internet in order to make innovative digital services. In combination with a user-centered design approach, they fundamentally alter the nature of the industry they operate in. Think Spotify for streaming music instead of buying CDs, Netflix in place of movie rentals and scheduled TV programming, or Airbnb for unique accommodation in place of hotels.

All of these brands are now considered as household names, such is their popularity. In no small part, this can be somewhat attributed to the focus they put on the needs of their customer. If you give your customers – your users – a better experience, something that enhances their lives, helps them to get their tasks done and to achieve their goals, and to align these needs with your business goals, the business will be successful.

Unfortunately, not all of us have the chance to be working for trailblazing companies such as Netflix, Spotify, Twitter, or any of the other digital disruptors that spring to mind. The vast majority of businesses in the world that have recognized the need to adapt are undergoing some kind of digital transformation program. This isn't only about improving their apps or websites, but improving all aspects of their current technology-based infrastructure, giving them the capability to pivot and move in new directions to provide for the needs of their customers. From my experience, from small- and medium-sized enterprises (SMEs) to large corporations with household brand names, an integral part of this digital transformation is to increase the level of UX maturity within the organization. You may well be aware of this going on around you in your workplace today.

Before we take a look at how businesses can utilize user-centered design to enhance the user experience, we have to understand where the organization lies in terms of its own level of UX maturity.

The Various States of UX Maturity

In my experience of working in the United Kingdom with SMEs and larger organizations that have been around for a decade or more, it is still common to find the business running on legacy systems that require in-depth knowledge and a significant amount of time to upgrade. There are also partnerships with third parties that provide a multitude of digital and product services. These organizations also tend to have a "less than nimble" approach to design and development of products and services. These are the organizations that are having the realization that they have to adapt to survive; that they must deliver not only outstanding products, but outstanding experiences to their customers.

Although user experience isn't a new concept, the discipline of user experience design can still be found to be immature in the vast majority of the types of organizations mentioned above. In 2017, I was not only working as the only user experience designer in a 250-employee strong organization, but I was also the first user experience designer that they had ever employed. Although we may see the vocal minority leading the way in user experience design by publishing articles, speaking at conferences, and sharing their process, it is naïve to think that all organizations now focus on user experience; we must not lose sight that the majority are still playing catch up.

Those organizations are beginning to truly understand the benefits of good user experience, and the user-centered design approach that is required in order to deliver it, but the culture of their organization is in need of a paradigm shift to be able to not only accommodate this new approach, but to place it at the core of everything the organization does.

There have been a number of models created against which an organization can measure itself with regard to their level of UX maturity, the most well-known of which would be Neilsen's UX Maturity Model (Figure 2-1). The model outlines eight stages of maturity ranging from "Hostility Toward Usability" to the "User-Driven Corporation."

Levels of UX Maturity			
	High	8	User–Driven Corporation
	High	7	Integrated User–Centred Design
	Medium	6	Systematic User–Centred Design Process
	Medium	5	Managed Usability
	Medium	4	Dedicated UX Budget
	Low	3	Skunkworks User Experience
	Low	2	Developer–Centred User Experience
	Low	1	Hostility Toward Usability

Figure 2-1. *Adapted from Neilsen's UX Maturity Model*

The Lower Levels of UX Maturity

The first three levels of the model focus around the business requirements and IT constraints, and these are the factors that drive the development of any given product or feature. The hostility toward usability means that the end users are essentially deemed irrelevant to the process, and the goal of the development team is to build features and make them work to the provided specifications. These organizations do not consider their users to be at the same level of importance as the strategic or financial needs of the company, as depicted in Figure 2-2.

Stage 2, the Developer-Centered User Experience, is largely an exercise in self-referential design. The internal project teams will rely on their own intuition and experience to decide what constitutes good usability, and this approach is only ever successful when the teams that are working on the project are the end users themselves.

When an organization hits stage 3, Skunkworks User Experience, there is now a realization that the organization can no longer rely on its internal teams to use their best judgment on what will constitute a good user experience, or what the most usable solution for their customers may be. The very beginnings of real user-centered design work begin to appear, but the efforts to involve users in the design of their products will still be few and far between.

A Low Level UX Maturity Organisation

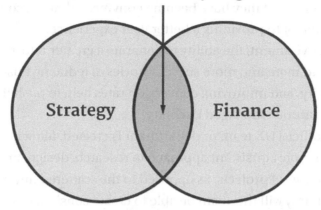

Figure 2-2. *A depiction of where an organization of low-level UX maturity sits within common driving forces of a business*

These lower levels of UX maturity are where many organizations find themselves today. This can be a somewhat difficult thing to comprehend, as the most vocal companies springing up in Silicon Valley and other tech bubbles are generally borne out of the needs of the user and find themselves at the higher levels of UX maturity from their inception.

As thought leaders in the digital world, in combination with how vocal they can be within the Silicon Valley bubble, the rhetoric of the digital disruptors can easily overshadow the millions upon millions of businesses that are still struggling through their own digital transformation programs with the aim of leveraging the same advantages that are intrinsic to those organizations that embrace the start-up culture: devolving responsibilities to product teams; an agile approach that encourages innovation; and the ability to pivot to suits the needs of the business, and more importantly, their customers.

The Medium Levels of UX Maturity

The medium levels of UX maturity, depicted as levels 4 through 6 in Neilsen's UX Maturity Model, begin to manifest an appreciation of the value of UX activities from the business, enough for them to create a dedicated UX budget. This tends to happen organically as the work done by the small and loosely structured team during the

Skunkworks User Experience stage has caught the eyes of some of those higher up in the organization's hierarchy, and they have become convinced that the company will profit from further investment into providing a better user experience.

With additional investment, the ability to generate a greater return over time becomes possible, and more and more success stories of reducing business costs, increasing productivity, and improving conversion rates help to push the organization to the 5th stage of UX maturity: Managed Usability.

At this stage, an official UX team or department is created, allowing the business to reap the benefits of a more consistent approach to research, design, and usability testing throughout a wider range of projects, as opposed to the scattered funding made available in levels 3 and 4. Not only will this team be able to create consistency, they will also have the remit to consider the user experience across the wider organization, as opposed to the more localized implementation of user experience at a project, or even department level. The leaders of this team will no longer be focused on the details – designing and implementing better solutions will be down to the members of the team – but will be working toward a higher purpose: to increase UX maturity to the levels where it is considered to be part of the business strategy.

Despite their being both a larger budget and remit than previous levels, it is still not possible to realize all of the potential user experience design activities for every project throughout an organization at any given time. Although the direction to create a more unified and universal approach to user experience design is in place, the implementation takes a large amount of time to gain traction throughout the business, meaning that the application of UX activities can still be largely fragmented.

Moving to level 6, Systematic User-Centered Design, we find that the organization looks to utilize user research before approaching design on their more important projects. The business also looks to measure the impact of user experience utilizing key performance indicators, along with other familiar methods used to measure the performance of other areas of the business. With the ability for the business to monitor the performance of each release, an iterative design process becomes more common as the business realizes that the best solution is hardly ever created at the first attempt, but that continuous improvements can be made over time, constantly improving the user experience, iteration after iteration.

The Higher Levels of UX Maturity

Upon reaching stage 7, Integrated User-Centered Design, everything within a project is driven by user data that comes from the now commonplace, and far more prominent, user research activities at project inception. The foundations laid in stage 6 for monitoring the user experience evolves to be able to produce valuable quantitative data that can be used to measure against usability goals based on user data. By Neilsen's definition, this is the "UX nirvana as far as interaction design goes," so why is there another stage beyond this?

The answer is that user experience doesn't have to be just part of the design domain but can influence the business in ways that completely transform how strategic decisions are made. User research doesn't just influence the direction of a project, it influences what projects the company should give the greenlight, what their priorities are, as well as the overarching strategic direction. User Experience becomes Customer Experience, covering larger aspects of service design for all touchpoints that customers have with the organization.

As of 2018, there are a relatively miniscule number of organizations in the world that have reached the highest levels of UX maturity. Although we are able to talk through the different levels of UX maturity in just a few pages of this book, the reality is that this process can take years, and more likely decades, depending on where your organization currently resides in this scale. The path to the higher levels of UX maturity is a long, winding, arduous journey, in which, eventually, pretty much everybody within an organization will require at least a basic understanding of the UX process since it will be part of their day-to-day way of working, engrained in the culture of the business. The result of this is that the users are seen as equal importance to the business as the strategic and financial elements of the business equation, as depicted in Figure 2-3 below.

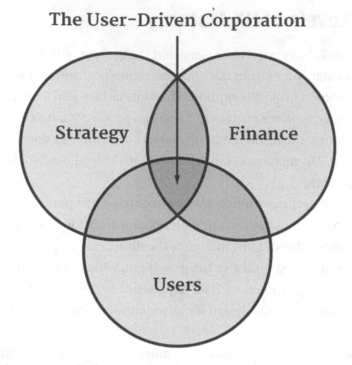

Figure 2-3. *A depiction of where a user-driven organization sits within equal driving forces of strategy, finance, and users*

Although it may not necessarily be the main goal when it comes to the digital transformation of an organization, the advancement through the stages of UX maturity is one of the most important advancements for the business. As the experience of the user becomes more central to organizational goals, the more engrained it becomes in their day-to-day operations.

The Costs Due to Lack of a User-Centered Design Process

Many organizations that haven't done much in the way of user-centered design, or even lent much thought to the user experience of their digital products, will often question the amount of work required in implementing a design process, let alone one that involves the users.

There will always be pressure applied from other business priorities, such as being first to market, or to hit internal deadlines for release windows. More often than not, with a less mature level of UX understanding, this design process can be under increasing pressure to legitimize its inclusion within the chain of delivery.

Ultimately the business will ask whether investing in user experience design is worth it.

"If you think good design is expensive, you should look at the cost of bad design."

– Ralf Speth

The business world is very much focused on numbers: profit margins, average order values, recurring revenues, customer lifetime values, et cetera. And so they should be. Without measuring the success and failures of past projects, how can they possibly learn from their mistakes, and in doing so, avoid repeating the same type of mistakes in the future?

The value of good design, however, can be much more difficulty to quantify in those terms, so we have to look to the business world to borrow models on which we can provide evidence that spending time and resources on design will reap the benefits in the longer term.

In organizations where design is not truly valued, it can be perceived as something that is more of an expense, and a costly one at that. This is also a reflection of the level of maturity in the field of UX that a business has.

A Real-World Example

When I joined an organization as their first and only UX Designer, there were a number of multipage forms that constituted different user journeys for each of the products or services that were being sold to their potential customers: a typical sales funnel for a business website selling their products to their potential customers.

One of the particular journeys that I got to work on was an out-of-the-box, white label solution for home insurance. In terms of design, the only changes that had been made to a fairly basic multipage form was the addition of the company logo, along with a change in color palette to reflect the brand. This particular online journey performed terribly. There were dropout rates of around 40% at every step of the journey, meaning that for every 100 visitors to our quote journey, only 8 would make it to the screen where they could buy an insurance policy.

The business was acutely aware that work needed to be done, so a project team was formed with the aim of creating a new front end that we would have more control over as a company, and no longer rely on a third party to deliver the digital journey on our behalf. However, this project did not initially contain any design phase at all as it was purely focused on re-creating the existing journey, but to be in our own domain of control.

After a few conversations and compromises with the project team and the senior management, we were able to integrate a four-week design phase into the project. This would consist of a great deal of analysis on the questions that comprised the journey and how they were organized, with three rounds of design, prototyping, and usability testing with real customers. Armed with the figures that the white label solution had generated for the business over the past years, in combination with some internal guerrilla testing of a very early prototype, the project team was able to create a set of objectives, key performance indicators, and targets that the business could sign off on.

Before the introduction of this design phase, there was no additional benefit to be gained from the first minimum viable product, other than having direct control over the journey to improve the turnaround for future iterations of the user journey. With the introduction of a user-centered design phase, we were able to propose a return on investment with our first release of a new user journey.

Within the first month of release of this new home insurance journey, we had smashed all of our projected targets out of the park. The number of policies sold went up 201% compared to the same period in the previous year, and the profit margin went up by more than 325%.

With just the introduction of a four-week design phase, we were able to create a huge benefit for the business, and all from a minimum viable product that we could launch for our customers.

User Experience Is No Longer an Optional Extra

The less concerned the organization is with the user experience, the more common it is for the design process to be brushed aside as an optional extra. Something that is not a core component of what the organization delivers to its customers.

In 2005, the Institute of Electrical and Electronics Engineers (IEEE) published a report entitled "Why Software Fails." The report contained a list of the 12 most common factors that contribute toward the failure of software projects:

- Unrealistic or unarticulated project goals

- Inaccurate estimates of needed resources

- Badly defined system requirements

- Poor reporting of the project's status

- Unmanaged risks

- Poor communication among customers, developers, and users

- Use of immature technology

- Inability to handle the project's complexity

- Sloppy development practices

- Poor project management

- Stakeholder politics

- Commercial pressures

The report estimated that organizations and governments would have spent $1 trillion that year on IT hardware, software, and services across the globe. Of the IT projects that were initiated, between 5 to 15% of them would be abandoned before or shortly after delivery, as they would have been deemed hopelessly inadequate.

Beyond that, it was estimated that 50% of a developer's time is spent reworking avoidable issues. Literally half of a developer's time was spent doing work that shouldn't be needed due to some of those factors listed above. The cost of fixing an error after development has been completed is 100 times that of fixing the error before development has been completed.

The CHAOS Report – an annual report generated from research by The Standish Group – stated in 2016 that 31.1% of projects were cancelled before they were completed, and 52.7% of projects would cost 189% of their original estimates.

Three of those factors listed in the IEEE report – specifically badly defined system requirements, poor communication among customers, developers, and users, and stakeholder politics – can be avoided by implementing some of the techniques that are common practice within user-centered design, such as user research, usability testing, and stakeholder interviews. Although these user-centered design activities can be of great benefit in these areas, they are not a magic wand that can be waved when things start to go awry; instead they must be utilized from the very beginning of a project in order to be effective.

By implementing user-centered design, we can help to prevent these issues that can cause immense frustration for developers (as well as the wider project team), we can negate some of the contributing factors, as well as the excessive associated costs to the business by reducing the risk of project failure. Not only can a user-centered design approach limit the risk for the business, and reduce costs, but it can also have a huge positive impact in terms of return on investment (ROI), effectively removing the barrier of increased costs up front to fund a user-centered design approach within a project.

The ROI of UX Design

"Usability goals are business goals. Websites that are hard to use frustrate customers, forfeit revenue, and erode brands."

– Forrester Research

The justification of the amount of work that needs to be undertaken through a user-centered design process can be difficult to measure in a way that the business can utilize effectively. As we mentioned earlier, business decisions revolve around numbers. The methodologies within user-centered design provides us with all kinds of data that proves what customers like and don't like, what they find easy to use, and whether the product helped them to complete their task or reach their goal.

But these facts and figures on their own don't relate to the concerns of the business. They need to be converted into a language that is understood and respected in the business world. They need to be converted into a metric: increase in conversion rate, reduction in abandonment, reduction in calls to the support staff, decrease in the amount of required training, increased product usage, reduction in development time, or a reduction in errors – all of which can be indicators of a successful UX design process that the business can measure.

Whatever the metric, there is a distinct business need to show that return on investment.

A Scenario for Calculating ROI

Let's imagine that our business is an insurance broker that has a call center with 200 sales staff. Every day, the sales staff collectively makes a number of errors when inputting the details of their customers into the system, throughout the working day. From this, in conjunction with some other data that we are already aware of, we can calculate the cost of these errors to the business.

(# of errors) × (Avg. repair time) × (Employee cost) × (# of employees)
= Cost savings

On average every user makes 2 errors per day when entering a customer's contact details, which equates to 10 errors per week, per employee. The average time for the employee to rectify each of those errors is 10 minutes. The employee cost, or the hourly rate that a member of the sales staff is paid, is $10, and we already know that we have 200 employees. So our calculation looks like this:

(10 errors/week) × (0.1666 hours) × ($10/hour) × 200 employees)

= $3,332/week

= $39,984/year

Now the business is aware of the cost of the problem, and how much can be saved if the problem is corrected. Against this, we can now measure the cost of using a user-centered design approach to resolve the problem. In order to remove the possibility of these errors occurring when an employee is entering these details, a designer will create a possible solution as a prototype, test this with users, and iterate on the proposed solution until a usable and successful solution is found.

This work for the designer is estimated at 40 hours, at the hourly rate of $20, which creates a total design cost of $800. We will also require some time from the sales staff for testing. For 3 rounds of testing with 6 users, with each test taking 30 minutes, the cost for these participants would total $90 for the 9 hours required. For the developers to implement this solution, work is estimated at 8 hours at an hourly rate of $15, creating a development cost of $120.

Therefore, the estimated total cost to remove the possibility of this error occurring for the sales staff is just $1,010. By implementing this change, the business can realize its investment in just over 1.5 days following implementation, which means the cost savings to the business over a year for this particular solution would be $38,974.

UX Is Everyone's Responsibility

One thing that is clear from the example above is that the input of both designers and developers was required to deliver a solution to a problem in order to benefit the business. The design team are not the only ones in a product or feature team who influence the user experience. People outside of the design team, or those that don't have the word "designer" in their job titles, make significant design choices, whether consciously or otherwise, that affect the resulting customer experience in a huge variety of ways.

Much has been said in the design community about what actually constitutes a designer. There are conflicting opinions from both sides of the argument, specific examples from a wide variety of experiences, and criteria banded around about what skills make a designer. I don't particularly want to get involved in that debate – although this book may have already committed me to a particular position on that front – but more importantly, I don't want developers to be drawn into that debate, nor anyone outside of what is considered the "design profession," for lack of a better categorization.

Regardless of whatever position you may take in this kind of debate, it doesn't change the fact that anyone who makes a decision on how something works within a digital product ultimately affects the resulting user experience.

Developers are at the sharp end when it comes to delivering a digital product. Almost every choice they make will have some kind of bearing on the resulting user experience; from big decisions on what architecture or framework to employ, down to the properties of individual elements on a screen such as how they handle micro-interactions, animations, accessibility, feedback mechanisms, and more. They are at the last point in the process where creative decisions are made that come together with all of the previous decisions that culminate in the resulting user experience.

The relevance of having the user in mind while making everyday decisions is just as important here as it is when we are defining what we are to build. If we don't consider the user at every stage, for every decision, and neglect to consider the needs of the user from inception to completion, there is nobody who can come along after the fact, wave a magic wand, and fix the resulting problems. There are so many factors to consider, such as accessibility issues, methods by which the user can interact with the product, how we set a user's expectation for what will happen next, to how we provide feedback so they know what has just happened; these, and many, many more considerations must be constantly contemplated to avoid the pitfalls that can result in a poorer user experience.

No one, at any given point in the project life cycle, should be exempt from considering the user; the importance of user experience is ubiquitous.

Summary

In this chapter we have touched on how user experience is viewed from a business perspective, and how this perception changes as the level of UX maturity grows within an organiz ation. We walked through these levels of maturity, illustrating how the role of user experience as a discipline, and its associated activities help to further the continued integration of a user-centered design approach.

We examined the costs where there is a lack of UX design along with a range of factors that lead to project failure and explored the return on investment that it can provide with some real-world and theoretical examples. Finally, we touched on why user experience is not just the responsibility of a "designer," and that anyone who makes a decision on how something works has an impact on the resulting user experience.

CHAPTER 3

Business Objectives vs. User Goals

In an ideal world, where we find ourselves in the highest levels of UX maturity within our organization, where we have reached the level of Integrated User-Centered Design, the disciplines of user experience are fully integrated with the everyday workings of the business. User goals are considered just as important as the business objectives, simply because they are one and the same. User research is best used to determine the direction of the business, to define its strategy, its products, and even have an influence beyond the digital aspects of the organization.

However, as we have already discussed in the previous chapter, very few of us indeed will work for an organization that functions at these higher levels of UX maturity. So what challenges arise for the rest of us who are striving to enrich the products we are working to deliver by bringing the various disciplines of user experience design to the table?

As much as I'd love to think that the goals of the user should come out on top every time – after all, it is they who we are designing and building our digital products for – this is simply not the case in the vast majority of organizations in the real world.

Being a champion for the user, to be the one who echoes their voice internally, is an everyday struggle with the ultimate aim being to get that voice heard above all of the other competing needs and constraints within any given project that you work on. Every aspect of a project is fighting to be heard over the others: user research, technical constraints, usability testing results, personal opinions, resource, budgets, et cetera. But one thing is always heard above all others and inevitably wins out: business objectives.

Part of being the voice of the user within an organization is to engage in these struggles, to identify the challenges and conflicts, and to look to resolve them by aligning user goals with the business objectives. But before we look into how we go about this, there's something that seems counterintuitive to the overarching theme of this book that we need to understand first.

© Westley Knight 2019
W. Knight, *UX for Developers*, https://doi.org/10.1007/978-1-4842-4227-8_3

Business Goals Transcend User Needs

As much as it pains me to put it down in writing, business goals are more important than the needs of the user. I know, this is a book championing UX and how other disciplines can embrace user-centered approaches, and here I am with a whole section saying that business goals are more important than user needs. It sounds like I'm not really fully invested in this user-centered design stuff, doesn't it? So, let's correct that now.

In order to create a successful digital user experience and a sustainable product, it must fulfill the objectives of the business. It needs to provide, not only a return on investment, but continuing profit for it to be seen as a sustainable part of the business. If the product does not fulfill this most basic of requirements, the product will cease to exist, meaning there will be nothing to design a user experience for.

Ultimately, meeting business objectives is the key to a successful product in the eyes of the organization we are designing and building this product for. What this means for the majority of us working internally is that the requirements of our projects are predominantly set by the business. C-level executives in the higher echelons of the organization will make strategic decisions to take the company forward to fulfill their long-term goals. These decisions then filter down through the chain of command, spawning ideas for projects and products that aim to fulfill these strategic goals in order to push the company forward.

One of the most prominent examples of such a strategic decision that springs to my mind is the story of Fab. In February of 2010, Fabulis – to give Fab its original full name – began life as a social network with a target audience of gay men. Unfortunately, the platform was less than successful, so in June of 2011 the co-founders decided to take the company in a completely different direction, selling handpicked clothes, accessories, and home goods. Five months following the relaunch, Fab had garnered 1 million members, reaching this number faster than Facebook and Twitter.

Although this is a particularly extreme example where an organization completely pivoted on their offering, it illustrates how and why these kinds of decisions are made for the strategic good of the company.

At this point of inception – where a new product is about to be conceived – user-centered design can have the biggest impact. If utilized correctly at this stage, it can dramatically reduce risk to the business, allowing early failure and valuable lessons to be learned without heavy investment in design and development. This essentially avoids time and effort being ploughed into something that could quite easily turn out to be an expensive mistake. It is here that user-centered design, and consideration of the user experience, can influence the direction that a product will take with the benefits of involving users in the design process.

However, a lack of maturity in terms of UX within an organization means that user-centered teams face the challenge of not being involved early enough in the process. That said, whenever the user-centered approach is adopted during the life cycle of a project, it would certainly have a positive impact going forward.

This almost retroactive, use of user-centered design is a symptom of the primary importance attached to business goals; other goals become secondary to them, almost becoming an afterthought. While meeting business objectives is key to a successful product, creating a better experience for its users will see it flourish.

Measuring Success

In order to measure the success of a product, the business world has many metrics against which performance can be measured that come in the form of things like Key Performance Indicators (KPIs) or Objectives and Key Results (OKRs).

Let's say that your product is an informational website. It could be measured by the number of unique visitors, number of returning visitors, time spent on the site, and a large variety of other pertinent metrics that can be pulled from tools like Google Analytics. In the case of an e-commerce site, you will likely have specific goals set around conversion rates, average order value, cart abandonment, et cetera.

Every single one of these metrics, regardless of the type of digital product under scrutiny, have one main characteristic in common: they can all be empirically measured. We can gather the data to see *exactly* how well any specific aspect of a product is performing, and the resulting figures can easily be communicated back to the business. The reason for this relative ease of communication is due to their similarity with metrics that are utilized in other areas of the business. The only difference is really the source from which these metrics originate; they come from a digital platform rather than from internal, offline teams such as sales or customer support.

The ability to define metrics against which the user experience can be is one of the biggest challenges arising from the adoption of a user-centered design approach. It is not enough for us simply to be concerned with the user experience, we have to push to implement our ideas and to try to influence proceedings to create a better resulting product, regardless of our position within the hierarchy of the project, or the wider organization. This is not something that only those with the UX acronym in their job title should be striving to do; anyone and everyone who is involved in creating a product that will be used by other human beings should be completely invested in the resulting product and the experience that it delivers to those people.

As we stated at the end of the previous chapter, developers are in a position to directly affect the resulting experience through their own decisions on their implementation of any given solution. As well as this, it is useful to bear in mind that in this era of digital technology, the experience of a user while using your product now holds much greater significance as to whether the product becomes successful or not than it did a decade ago.

Although you may not consider yourself, or your role, to be able to influence the user experience of your product for the better, then you are, quite simply, selling yourself short. The knowledge, skills, and tools that you utilize on a daily basis are the channel through which all the strategic decisions, designs, and requirements must flow to bring a digital product to life. As a developer, you aren't expected to handle any of the aspects of a user-centered design process, and neither should you be, especially when you may already have a UX designer within your team. But your expertise, your knowledge of the existing frameworks and platforms, of new advances in technology, of how to turn ideas and designs and requirements into usable, functional products; that is what separates you from the other roles in your team, that is your value, that is what you bring to the table.

Everyone in the team must have to be able to effectively communicate the value that a user-centered design approach can provide to the business, and this has to be done on an equivalent level of scale and clarity to those metrics that are so well utilized from other areas of the business.

In order to evaluate a user-centered approach to design, we need to show the business what value it will deliver; what will be the return on investment?

Defining Business Objectives

Let's start by taking a look at how we set and measure business objectives. One of the most common ways to define business objectives is to use SMART goals. The origins of this method are most commonly attributed to the "Management by Objectives" approach that was published by Peter Drucker in his 1954 book, *The Practice of Management* (HarperCollins). SMART is an acronym for the five key elements required to set clear and attainable business goals:

1. Specific - target a specific area for improvement.

2. Measurable - quantify an indicator of progress.

3. Achievable - the goal must be attainable.

4. Relevant - the goal must be important to the business.

5. Time-related - a deadline by which to reach the goal.

Let's take a look at an example of a SMART business goal, and how this may work for a hypothetical business.

> *Bella's Vintage is a fictional e-commerce site that specializes in selling vintage clothing. During the month of June, the business is aiming to sell 20% more evening dresses than last year as this one of the most popular months for weddings in the UK.*

This statement holds everything that is required for it to qualify as a SMART goal. Here's how parts of that statement align to each of the SMART criteria:

1. Specific - Increase sales of evening dresses.

2. Measurable - By number of sales.

3. Achievable - A 20% rise is not out of the question.

4. Relevant - Sales are always important to business!

5. Time-related - Specified as the month of June.

This business goal ticks all of the boxes, and as a result gives everyone involved a clear understanding and direction needed to achieve the goal.

Defining User Goals

User goals are defined rather differently to business objectives. One of the most common ways to define user goals is by utilizing User Stories. These are short sentences – which tend to be shorter than a SMART business goal statement – that describe what type of user someone is, the goal they want to achieve, and why they want to achieve it. They generally follow this structure:

> *As an [actor], I want [action] so that [achievement].*

We can flesh this out into a possible user story in the context of the Bella's Vintage example we used to create our business objective:

> *As a wedding guest, I want to buy a beautiful evening dress so that I can look and feel amazing.*

In order to convince the business that these user stories can contribute toward the more strategic business goals, that they can have a positive effect on the numbers they care about, we need to look at ways in which we can measure user stories so that they can be considered to be of equal importance as the existing business goals.

Many businesses utilize user stories as part of an Agile software development approach, which can provide us with a framework that provides us with additional aspects to a user story when compared to the comparatively basic version when simply defining a user's goal.

The first of these additions is acceptance criteria. Acceptance criteria define the boundaries of a user story and are used as the yardstick against which we measure if a story has completed. For example, some of the acceptance criteria for our Bella's Vintage user story could be:

- *User must be able to find an item in their desired category.*

- *User must be able to add a selected item to their basket.*

- *User must be able to review their basket.*

- *User must be able complete the payment/checkout process.*

- *User must receive confirmation of purchase.*

These acceptance criteria now provide us with elements of a user story that both provide the developer with everything they need to successfully deliver against a user story, with the added benefit to the business that the outcome of the delivery is measurable.

By following through on the initial user story – fleshing out the requirements through acceptance criteria and delivering within the time constraint of a predefined sprint in an Agile development process – developers are able to deliver real, measurable value to the business from what started out as a user story, rather than an internally focused business goal. All of this helps the wider business become more user centered in their approach to design and development.

Making Business and User Goals Work Together

In the majority of cases, you will find that user goals and business objectives complement each other, which is also an indicator that the organization is focused on its customers and delivering products that work for them and that will benefit the business.

There are, however, some occasions where user goals will conflict with the business objectives. For example, in financial institutions that are regulated by the Financial Conduct Authority (FCA) in the United Kingdom, there are a number of legally required documents that must be presented to a user when in the process of applying for a credit card. One of these documents is the Standard European Consumer Credit Information (SECCI), which allows the prospective customer to compare one card against another in terms of the key features, borrowing costs, rates of interest, and many more aspects.

Essentially, it's one of those really long, legal-sounding documents that you know you should read as the person applying for a credit card, but ultimately, as a user, you just want to click the button to finish your application.

This is a typical case of business objectives conflicting with user goals. Once a user has made a decision on the product they want, in order to help that user complete the process that results in them attaining their goal – in this case, applying for a credit card – we should remove every possible obstacle to help them get to that goal in a timely and efficient manner. The SECCI feels like an obstacle to the user. It's a large and complicated hoop that they must jump through in order to reach their goal.

This is actually a fantastic example of why business objectives trump user goals. An improved user experience – one that purely focuses on the user and their aims to complete their goal in this case – would look to avoid the user hitting this perceived hurdle in favor of a slicker path to completion. This approach could lead to a lack of information provided to the user that would help them make an informed choice about the product they wish to apply for. It could also lead to costly repercussions for the user down the line if they were not presented with alternative choices that may be better suited to their situation.

From a business perspective, the legal and financial repercussions can also be huge if the institution fails to follow the legal guidance and requirements.

There are many more examples where some business objectives are not necessarily absolute must-have items, but the benefits they can give to the business could possibly outweigh the negative impact on the user experience.

A simple example of this would be marketing questions contained within a registration form. They may not be mandatory fields but can provide a great deal of insight into the user who registers, but on the other hand it's another field that the user has to fill in to complete the registration process. This is where you have to strike a balance between a slicker user experience in a form that contains less fields for the user to complete, and the value gained by the business when users do fill out the additional details.

Striking the Balance

The best way of truly achieving alignment between user goals and business objectives is to grow the level of UX maturity in your organization to the point that they achieve parity in terms of their strategic value. However, this period of transition can take many years, but there is a lot of work to be done in the meantime.

For those organizations that are starting to embrace UX, the best way to begin aligning user goals and business objectives is for us to start treating them with the same level of gravitas, to consider the goals of the user to be on equal terms with the goals of the business. It's a "fake it 'til you make it" approach. The more we can do to reduce the disparity between user goals and business objectives – in terms of both importance and understanding – the more the business will allow the project teams to spend the more time, effort, and resources on creating a better user experience while still aiming to fulfill the business objectives.

Summary

In this chapter, we have looked at the challenges we face when trying to bring user goals to the same level of importance as the business goals within an organization. Although the goals of the business will always be top priority, we looked at how we could measure the success of our work, both in terms of value to the business and to the user, and how we can look to place them on a more equal footing by utilizing similar techniques to communicate value. Finally, we walked through a real-world example to show how we can make business goals and user goals complement each other, leading to successful implementations that benefit both the business and the user.

CHAPTER 4

Adjusting the Developer Perspective

As a developer, your day-to-day work will be heavily influenced by the business and is – more often than not, in my experience, working as a developer both in-house and in external agencies – viewed as a production line that churns out the code. The goal of that production line is to deliver against the business goals, with a concentration on efficiency, delivering to release windows, and can, in some cases, be treated as a commodity by product owners or the organization at large.

This is a symptom of the lower levels of UX maturity we discussed in Chapter 2. There can be hostility toward user experience and what it entails, simply as the organization has not yet come to the point at which it values the input of the users regarding the software they are creating, prioritizing their own internal goals above all else, and favoring self-referential design.

This kind of organizational culture – common in long-standing organizations that are still working toward digital transformation – places developers in silos, preventing any kind of exposure to the user and to user feedback, robbing any member of a development team of the chance to create some semblance of empathy toward the user and their needs.

Developers effectively "ran the show" when it came to building digital solutions for businesses a few years back. Software development was much more of a dark art, shrouded in mystery for those who were not so technologically minded. More recently however, as new technology and digital approaches are adopted, and are ever-increasingly becoming an integral part of everyday workings of organizations throughout the world, the metaphorical fog that had previously surrounded the internal application of software has dispersed. The personal adoption of new technologies, especially through mobile devices, has quickly changed the understanding of what is possible with

37

© Westley Knight 2019
W. Knight, *UX for Developers*, https://doi.org/10.1007/978-1-4842-4227-8_4

the technology that is now widely available. Non-developers within your organization now have a much greater understanding of what they want in regard to their digital projects, but not necessarily how to go about achieving those goals.

Just as businesses are now looking to take control of their futures by embracing the possibilities of digital advances, developers must now look outside of the confines of writing code to embrace a wider view of what it means to build applications, websites, and other software.

This chapter will look at how developers need to adjust the way they look at their role in creating digital products, and that they must expand their horizons in order to stay relevant in the evolving and maturing environments that will only grow more focused on user experience in the future.

Developer Decisions Impact the User Experience

Although a front-end developer will have the vast majority of their work seen and utilized by the users, it must not be underestimated how much every aspect of software, web, and app development can impact the user experience.

Depending on what kind of developer you are, whether you work on back-end systems that no user ever interacts directly with, if you build middleware or APIs that feed the relevant information into the front end, or if you work directly on the interfaces that your everyday users will interact with, you will have varying levels of impact on a user experience.

The back-end developer, working on core system functions – far from the minds and interactions of the user – can have a significant impact on their experience. Let's think about a developer who does a lot of work with databases. Regardless of the type of database, the queries that are run against the database to select, insert, update, or delete records within can have a significant impact on the front end, which translates into part of a user's experience.

If we imagine a database with a few million records sitting in the background, and, on the front end, we have a search box that allows users to search the full set of records for a keyword in a particular column. An inefficient query on the database could essentially grind the back-end systems to a halt and create a negative experience for the user having to wait for an inordinate amount of time for what should be a simple set of results from their point of view.

Creating a more intelligent process that improves the efficiency of the query, that allows vast amounts of records to be searched almost instantaneously by the user, and you have not only created a more efficient system, but a far superior user experience.

A solid foundation on which to build a user experience is paramount. It is this area where the lines are most blurred between the user experience and the functionality of a system. At this level, a solid foundation that provides all of functionality to cater to the user's needs – both current and future – will underpin the success of all of the user-centered decisions made from here on out.

It is very easy to think that there is a correlation between the level of impact that different levels of the same system will have against the user experience. Although developers working on the user interface elements will have a much more visible and direct impact on the user, it should not disguise the fact that every element of a system contributes to the overall user experience. The best user interface in the world will not save the experience of a slow and inefficient system that doesn't deliver to the needs of the user.

Developers Make Design Decisions Every Day

Let's take a moment and think about the last piece of work you did. As a developer, more likely than not, you made some kind of decision over how you implemented a specific element within that piece of work. For argument's sake, let's say you were working on a section of content that utilized some icons. You chose to use PNG files exported from the design files provided by the designer, but you also considered using an icon font, or perhaps SVG. The point is, it came to you to make that decision, and you had control over that decision as the authority on which way it was best to implement this particular piece of work.

A product owner, business analyst, subject matter expert – or someone else who doesn't have the word "designer" in their job title – will have made similar decisions in similar projects on a daily basis, or perhaps multiple times a day.

Any decision that is made by someone that affects how the item being created looks or functions is, by definition, a design decision.

> *Design (verb)*
>
> *To decide upon the look and functioning of an object.*

You can do a quick Google search for "everyone is a designer" and find a seemingly endless stream of opinion pieces on whether or not someone is a designer due to the influence or impact they have on the resulting product, or whether design should be left to "the designers," and even that none other than classically trained designers shall tread foot upon the hallowed ground of design.

Regardless of your own opinions, my own, or those of others on this matter, it cannot be ignored that decisions that impact the design of a digital product can be made by any and every individual that contributes to its creation.

Design happens regardless of whether a designer was involved or not, and this kind of accidental design is what we should be trying to avoid.

Wider Benefits of Adopting a User-Centered Approach

From the previous chapters in this book, we have already covered what user experience is and why it is important, mainly from the viewpoint of the digital product and the business behind it, and how a good user experience contributes the continued success of that product.

The benefits aren't just apparent for the business and the user, but also for the team that works to create the product, especially the developers.

By understanding what users need from the product you are building from the outset, you will reduce the risk of creating something that does not cater to the needs of your user, and you will have guidance from your user around the features and functions that they need from your product that will provide value to them. By detecting usability issues earlier in the development cycle, it has been found possible to cut development time by up to 50%. As a more extreme example, researched carried out by Human Factors International with American Airlines found that correcting usability earlier in their process, curing the design phase, that they reduced the costs of fixes to their internal systems by 60–90%.

In the white paper "Usability: A Business Case," Susan Weinshenck writes that in one rather famous study: "once a system is in development, correcting a problem costs 10 times more than fixing the same problem in design. If the system has been released, it costs 100 times more relative to fixing in design."

Without a user-centered approach to software design and development, most of a developer's time can be spent on maintenance of a digital product that has already been released, rather on the more important aspect of developing the features and products themselves. In this kind of scenario – in an organization with a lower level of UX maturity – most of the time and costs absorbed by the developers in their day-to-day work can be attributed to unforeseen user requirements, or usability issues, which were never discovered in the early phases of a project due to the lack of user involvement in the design process.

So, an established and thorough discovery phase – implementing user research, prototyping, usability testing, and various other user-experience design techniques – can bring huge savings in development costs and more robust requirements from the outset. In conjunction with a more iterative approach to both design and development, developers can influence the direction of the product, push to build things that are more interesting, and create work that has more impact for both the user and the business.

The Circles of Influence and Concern

Have you ever found yourself in a situation where a higher-level executive of your organization appears in one of your meetings or a stand-up one day, and proceeds to drop a metaphorical hand grenade in the middle of your project? Seemingly on a whim, your project has to pivot in a new direction based on little or no information, you're told the project is on hold, or that the whole thing has been canned? I want to talk about how you can better understand these kinds of situations, and how to only worry about those things we can control and influence.

You have the ability as a developer to offer valuable insight and experience throughout your team, and even more widely throughout your organization; it's just a question of how much you want to be able to influence the projects that you work on. In my opinion, a more integrated, respected, and understood developer will benefit the team, the product, and the user immeasurably.

In order to able to influence the seemingly external factors that impact your day-to-day work, you will need to gain an understanding of where these various elements sit in relation to your position as a developer in a team or the wider organization. By understanding the relationships between yourself and the members of your product team, development team, designers, and other members of your organization, you can learn to deal with the different challenges that arise when working on digital products.

Figure 4-1 is adapted from Stephen R. Covey's *7 Habits of Highly Effective People* (Free Press, 1989) and depicts the different levels of influence that you have over any given situation.

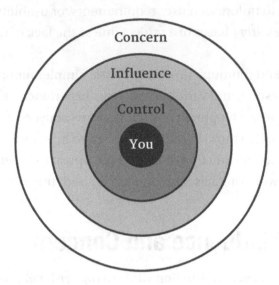

Figure 4-1. *The sphere of influence*

At the center is you, and immediately surrounding you is your area of control. For a developer, this will cover aspects of your work such as the code you write, and the development decisions you make as you go along. You have direct control over these decisions, and they are yours to make as the individual implementing the solution.

The next circle as we move outward is that of influence. These are the areas in which you have some level of input and can affect the outcome indirectly as the decision sits in the area of control of another individual. For example, you may put forward ideas to the product owner who can take the proposal on boards, or maybe request additional data of a third party who provides you with an API. Whatever the scenario may be, and regardless of your requests and suggestions, whether or not they are considered and implemented is not directly within your control, and lies with those whom you can only try to convince.

Finally, there is the circle of concern, which is where decisions get made that you have no influence over at all. This can be seen when high levels of management have made strategic decisions, and as the effects of these decisions filter down through the layers of the organization, can profoundly impact the way in which people then do their job.

This is by no means a fixed representation of how things stand with you and your various levels on influence. The amount of control and influence that you have over various aspects of a project will fluctuate over time and will change due to a number of factors, from variations within the organization to those within teams, and, most importantly, because of the actions you take in regard to your circle of influence.

As we mentioned at the beginning of this section, you have the ability as a developer to offer valuable insight and experience throughout your team, and even more widely throughout your organization. Involving yourself in the wider conversation surrounding the products you work on makes you more known and visible, and with a little bit of work, can give you a little more influence over more than just your own work.

We'll take a look at the specific tools and techniques you can utilize to grow your circles of both influence and control: perhaps even be able to gain influence over some elements in your circle of concern. In later chapters, we can still examine the areas in which you will be able to grow your influence and control, armed with what you will learn from this book.

Developer Experience Is Second to User Experience

In the earlier days of my career as a developer, before I became more aware of user experience and how my own focus needed to shift to those people that used what I would be building, it was very easy for me to get caught up in the everyday wrangling of writing code in a team of fellow developers. Even when working solo on projects, I would still be more concerned about how other developers, and once I was no longer around, would they be able to pick up my code, understand it, and continue to work on it and move things forward.

If you are now as I was back then, concerned about how your fellow developers will be able to understand and build upon the work that you have done, you are already thinking about user experience, just with a slightly different focus trained toward your developer colleagues.

This is a fantastic place to be as you look to begin your journey into understanding user experience design, and it offers a good foundation for you to expand your perspective with regard to what you're building, and who you are building it for.

Although this a good place to start, there is one main hurdle that you will have to overcome in order to cultivate a more user-focused perspective to your work: the experience you are able to give other developers as users of the code that you write pales into insignificance to the experience of the people who use the products you build.

This wasn't a simple and straightforward realization for me, and one that I in no way came to quickly. I took me years to evolve this understanding before it really hit me and I began to change how I thought about the solutions I was building, and who I was building them for. My realization came during a project for a theme park, specifically in rebuilding the page from which users would buy their tickets. There was no organization to the options from which you could choose; all-day passes were mixed in with individual ride tickets, along with annual passes, online exclusives, each with a variation on price for children, adults, and pensioners. If you were to make a mental list in your head of all of these options now, you would probably group them by ticket type: individual, day pass, annual pass. Or perhaps you would list them in age groups; child, adult, pensioner. Neither of these were true, it was just a seemingly random list with no discernible order to the items within. It just so happened that I had my own young family at the time, and had been to this park on many occasions, but had always paid on the door. I wondered how frustrating and confusing this must be for nontechnical people: potential park visitors with children who just wanted to take them out for a day of fun, but were instead confronted with an awful experience, before they had even arrived at the park. Just by asking around the office, by involving other people – other potential users with young families – we quickly found a better way of approaching a solution than if we were only to rebuild that which already existed on a newer platform. From this point on, there was no looking back for me, this was the only way in which we should be building things: building them for the people that use them.

Hopefully, in reading this, you will come to a similar realization with more haste than me. By extending your thoughts beyond your fellow developers to those end users, what seems like a huge change in mindset is actually something that is easily managed. By bringing the end users from your circle of concern (or even from outside of that circle) into your circle of influence, by making it part of what affects the work that you do, you will have made the biggest step toward becoming a user-focused developer.

Design Competency

Without trying to turn any developers who read this from becoming an out-and-out designer, the decisions you make that impact the design of the product you are creating should be made with some level of competency, and a level of understanding. A change in code can impact functionality, which, in turn, impacts the end user. The ability to anticipate what the impact your decisions will have on the user is what's important.

A similar argument seems to be ever surrounding the digital design community on whether designers should be able to code, and again, you'll find many varied opinions on this subject. In the case of that particular supposition, the concept can be boiled down to the fact that a digital designer doesn't have to know code, but it certainly helps in their understanding of the medium for which they design.

The same applies from the other side of the fence. Although a developer doesn't have to know design, it certainly helps them contribute toward making a better, more usable, and polished product.

Another benefit of becoming more well-versed in terms of design is that it creates another facet of your skillset, one that helps you integrate more fully into the team, and one that makes you a far more valuable asset to any given project, team, or organization. Again, it's not about becoming a fully-fledged designer, or about stepping on the toes of the designers you already work with, but to become more aware of what the design process involves, and how you can have a positive impact upon that process.

Putting People Before the System

Most of the concerns of the modern-day developer focus on efficiencies. Typically, as a front-end developer, I would be concerned about the small tweaks that I could make to improve the efficiency of my code so that it would render in the browser more quickly. For instance, I could vastly reduce the number of lines in a CSS file by utilizing the cascade, and by following the DRY (Don't Repeat Yourself) principle. This kind of work would result in smaller files for the browser to download and parse, and with these faster loading and execution times, there would be an increase in the performance of the website that I was working on.

My focus was on making the website more efficient, to reduce the amount of code. To create something efficient for the sake of efficiency. But there was actually far greater value in that kind of work that I hadn't really thought about at that time, and that was the benefit to the users.

Sometimes the byproduct of work that you put in to make something better for the system also benefits the user. However, in some cases the opposite can be true.

Let's consider something that is quite a bugbear of mine: error messages.

One of the most common issues I have come across with error messages is that the message displayed is either extremely unhelpful, or even worse, laying the blame at the foot of the user.

When we are creating validation rules, from the perspective of the developer, the foremost concern is that the data we submit to the system is in the correct format, ensuring that nothing breaks the underlying system. Adopting this mindset that puts the system first is critical to creating a robust system that can deliver the expected functionality to the user. However, the trap we must avoid is neglecting to think about the user who will be interacting with the system.

Figures 4-2 and 4-3 show two examples of some software giving completely unhelpful error messages that are, at best, just plain confusing to the everyday user.

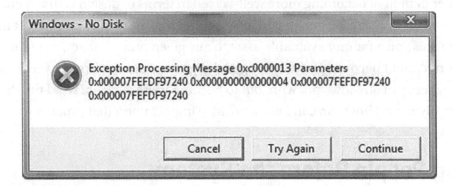

Figure 4-2. *An awful message from some Windows software*

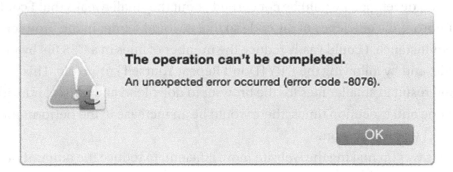

Figure 4-3. *An equally unhelpful message from some Apple software*

These error codes displayed in the user interface may be useful to developers while they're debugging their code, but to display these to a user gives them a sense of inferiority: that it's their fault that they don't know how to go back and fix whatever problem occurred and complete the task they were attempting.

Good error messages tell the user what went wrong in plain, concise language, and guide them about what to do next.

This is not a situation in which the quality of code is negatively affected by this kind of change; it actually provides the opportunity to create a better solution for both the developer and the user. Rather than a nondescript error stating "An unexpected error occurred (error code -8076)", we could tell the user exactly what the problem was, and what they can do to rectify it; "Sorry, we were unable to save the document, please try again." At the same time, we can also record the error in a way that is beneficial to the developer, perhaps by writing the error code that serves more purpose to the developer in an error log, or integrating into their tests.

This is just one example of where putting the people who use the system before the system itself can be beneficial in terms of creating a better user experience, without necessarily impacting negatively on the developer experience.

Making the Complex Simple

Rather than focusing on our user for a moment, let us consider your fellow developers as users. They will be working on the same code base as you, so you will likely be taking into consideration the needs of those other developers, the needs of the team. Essentially you are considering the user experience of those who will interact with the work you have done, you will look to create toward creating a simpler way of working together, removing points of friction, reducing complexity – not of the product itself, but of how it is built – and creating a common understanding that ensures that all the developers involved are on the same page when it comes to how they are building the product or feature they have been tasked to build with you.

As a developer, reducing the complexity of code is part of the job. Creating something more efficient and easier to maintain to only reduces technical debt, but it helps other developers gain a better understanding of the code itself. Even when we focus predominantly on the system and its efficiency, we can also be aiding the end users without having to apply a significant amount of additional effort, which would – and still will be under certain circumstances – otherwise be seen as inefficient.

Extending this concept of considering your fellow developers as users of the work you do – to those people who become users of the resulting product or feature – isn't taking too much of a cognitive leap when you frame it in this way, although the way in which the users interact with the different levels of the product – as in fellow developers compared to the product users – can be quite disparate.

For a user experience designer, this is a much easier concept to come to terms with, simply because the work we are already doing revolves around making things easier for the end user, and not just those that we work with internally on a project. The more time, effort, and thought we put into the solutions we design, the more likely the resulting product will be successful when adopted by the people who have a task or goal that the product helps them to complete.

Maintaining a Flexible Perspective

Being aware of the user, and keeping them in mind for the decisions you make on a day-to-day basis, is key to creating more usable products, and therefore better experiences for the user. There is a balance that must be struck so as to not dilute the skills and approaches you have learned to utilize to great effect in your time as a developer. It is possible to create better experience for user, and a better experience for your fellow developer at the same time by creating more impactful products with better code.

However, this balance can become more difficult to maintain the longer you work on a particular product or feature. The more you work on a particular aspect of a product, the more of a Subject Matter Expert (SME) you become. The more of an SME you become, the harder it is for you to set aside your level of knowledge on a particular aspect for you to envisage how a user may experience the product you are creating.

Figure 4-4 provides an illustrated example of the discrepancy between the understanding of a developer who is working on this particular product over a period of time, against that of the user who will have far less exposure to the inner workings of the product, and will very likely spend less time understanding how it works.

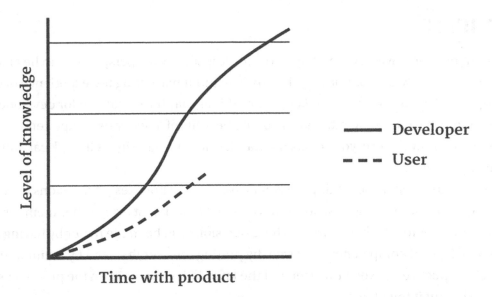

Figure 4-4. *A graph comparing the knowledge of developers and users gained in a particular product against the time spent working with it*

As you are in the process of building out a product, your understanding of the product deepens, and your expertise in the subject matter grows. You have a unique window into how everything works under the hood, how it all connects together; this gives you a huge opportunity to make a product that is much better, simply by shifting focus a little bit.

A user has none of this insight.

To expect that everyone else will have the same knowledge that you do when they first pick up something that they have never seen or used before is inherently ridiculous, and yet, I have found myself in that very same position as a developer. I could not grasp how difficult it may have been for the user, because it was nigh on impossible for me to understand how this worked for them, from their perspective.

The burden of the knowledge that I had gained over the time working on the product proved too much for me to easily switch my viewpoint to envisage the struggles that these users would be experiencing from the first time they would use the product I had built.

But if we can keep our users in mind throughout our development process, to constantly jump back to their perspective, as we become more of an expert in what we are building, we are still able to keep in touch with those who are not, we can maintain a certain level of empathy and understanding with our users.

Summary

In this chapter we have examined how we can adjust our own perspectives to be able to consider the user within our day-to-day work, without neglecting the experience of our developer colleagues. We have looked at how things may have changed for developers as organizations have become more aware of the benefits of a better user experience, and we have seen how the everyday decision that developers make in their work can impact that user experience.

Without developers becoming designers, we showed how design decisions are made every day, not just by designers, but by developers, and almost every other member of the teams within which they work. These decisions can be made better by having at least some level of competency in design, by putting the user first, and by maintaining a flexible perspective between the user and the knowledge you have on the product as the person who put it together.

CHAPTER 5

The Importance of Communication

The role of a developer is never simple or easy. The constant evolution in terms of best practice, newer and better frameworks appearing all of the time, and all this is moving at such a rapid pace that it makes Moore's Law look slow in comparison.

But hand in hand with these advancements in how developers go about their day-to-day work comes a vast ocean of information in the form of online courses, blog posts, tutorials; and more than enough to cover any particular development topic in which you may wish to advance your skill set. But the focus of all this information specializes in the advancement of technical skills for developers. Although there are many articles across the internet that will aid you with other, nontechnical skills, they are much harder to learn in this format as there aren't really any specifically quantifiable results.

If you take an online course to learn something like Vue, React, or Angular, you may well learn the framework during the process of creating an application. You have a measurable goal in that once you have applied the techniques you have learned throughout the course, you have a tangible result in the application you have created. But the improvement of your soft skills – and in particular your communication skills – can only really be improved through experience.

But why should you consider improving your communication skills? You may be a technically accomplished developer, but you may still be thought of as stereotypically introverted and difficult to deal with by others within your organization. This may not be a reflection on you as an individual, but will often be based on that stereotype, or perhaps even an individual's previous experience with developers who may have perpetuated that stereotype. However this perception may have formed, there is really only one way to change it, and that is by improving your ability to communicate with your wider team, outside of the comfortable embrace of your fellow developers.

W. Knight, *UX for Developers*, https://doi.org/10.1007/978-1-4842-4227-8_5

In juxtaposition to those more technical skills, improving your communication – by which I'm referring to the way in which you interact with the non-developer members of your team and stakeholders – only comes through the experience acquired over time as you evolve your understanding of team dynamics and individuals by a continuous process of trial and error.

Learning a Different Type of Skill

Development, programming, coding – or whatever the label it is given – is predominantly interaction between a human and a computer. This is where the vast majority of the time developers spend doing their job is thought to be. But, as Bob Dylan once sang, "the times they are a-changin'." In the journey to becoming a better developer in a world where user experience is gaining traction as both the driving force and the differentiator for most organizations and their products, the ability to relate to other people, to understand both their motives and their needs, requires far more dedication than it does to learn the next big framework. Depending on how you handle these kinds of interactions with other individuals, it may even require you to change your own behavior in the different ways we will look at in this chapter.

This is by no means a small task, regardless of whether or not you need to adjust your own behavior, and it can raise the question of why you should make the effort to communicate more effectively. It's certainly not easy to see the benefits you will gain from improving this particular skill, certainly not when compared to acquiring new programming skills.

In the vast majority of possible scenarios, you will be tasked with building something that is created by people, for people. In order to be able to make the right decisions for these people at both ends of this spectrum – from stakeholder to user – you need to understand what fulfills their needs, and that those needs far outweigh your own needs. It's all well and good that you may have a grand vision that you want to follow through from the outset, but if that doesn't align with the goals of satisfying both your stakeholders and your users, then it becomes an obstruction to achieving the goals that matter. And yes, those are the goals of the business and of the users, not necessarily your personal ones.

However, if the satisfaction of fulfilling the goals of the stakeholders and the users is simply not enough for you, there are benefits for the developer who learns to communicate more effectively. Being able to interact with and understand the needs of your non-developer colleagues, and act upon them accordingly, can break down the long-standing stereotypes that developers are very introverted beings that only interact well with their non-organic counterparts. Even the effort to simply communicate with people directly can be the stimulus that raises your profile and promotes you to a more valuable member of the team in the eyes of your colleagues. You become easier to work with; an avenue through which solutions to problems are offered, removing blockers rather than creating them due to technical constraints, or perhaps the additional workload required for a particular solution to a user's problem. At the very least, a more open line of communication with your product team is one thing that benefits you directly as a developer, and even if you are looking at this from a self-serving perspective, it still benefits the team as a whole.

Developer Insight Is an Essential Ingredient

Unfortunately, it can be a rather common occurrence that developers within a team are often the last people to be involved in design discussions of a project that they will be working on. I have experienced this from both sides of the fence, being excluded from any of the design discussions as a developer and only becoming involved when something needs to be built; and as a designer when the wider design team did not value the input of the developers when it came their knowledge and skill set, and the impact that it could have on the design.

As a project evolves from its initial conception, through approval, and into implementation, the make-up of the team slowly evolves to accommodate the requirements of each stage of the Software Development Life Cycle (SDLC). This is where a certain type of problem arises. Oftentimes the people who are required to develop the solution in the immediacy are brought into the team at that specific point.

For example, in the worst-case scenarios that I have experienced, the Business Analyst is drafted in during the evaluation phase of the SDLC to perform a feasibility study, or within the analysis phase to engage with stakeholders and to gather requirements. Designers and architects are then drafted in to work on the design phase. Only when the implementation phase comes around does the team think about engaging with the developers.

Essentially, this is too little, too late. All of the work carried out throughout the analysis and design phases, prior to the implementation phase, can benefit from the insight and experience of the developers.

This level of inclusion shouldn't only be reserved for the developers who would traditionally be involved toward the latter stages of the SDLC, but to all disciplines that are commonly excluded until requirements have been gathered. All of the disciplines within a project team will have valuable input to any given project, if only due to their different perspectives. Without the knowledge of other members of the team – architects, designers, developers, copywriters, etc. – there can be a distinct lack of foresight that could uncover a multitude of problems even before the design phase begins in earnest. Think back to the examples we used in Chapter 4 where we found that correcting a problem once a product is in development cost 10 times the amount to fix, or 100 times more after release, than if it were addressed in the design phase.

The value to be gained applies most vehemently to a developer's insight. The knowledge of their domain and the experience they have garnered throughout their careers, is the most underutilized component in a team that can deliver astonishing value when brought in to earlier phases of the SDLC. The amount of time and money saved by simply having knowledgeable developers in the room for discussions in the early stages of analysis can have a huge positive impact on the project.

This isn't simply down to their knowledge of the domain and their understanding of technical restraints that will eventually need to be considered, but their knowledge of technology outside of what is currently implemented can open up fascinating new avenues to explore that would never have been conceived, let alone considered without their input.

A Set of Guiding Principles for Better Communication

The value of including developers and other members of the team in earlier stages of the SDLC is the varying perspectives that can be brought to the table. You should never assume that anyone else in the team arrives at the table with the same knowledge that you have. Nothing is obvious. With this in mind, there are a few principles that are worth following in order to become a better communicator within your team.

Regardless of how good a communicator you may think you are, the dynamics and make-up of the teams that you work with will constantly be shifting, so it's no good to simply approach communication as a one-time thing. The more challenging aspects of communication between colleagues occurs when you step outside of your familiar surroundings, from out of your developer bubble, and into conversations with people who are no less intelligent than yourselves but not as technically savvy. Just as we discussed how you must be able to adapt your own perspective to consider your users in the last chapter, in this chapter we need to understand our colleagues more effectively.

Encouragement Trumps Criticism

Criticism is generally a demotivating judgment upon others. It is an extremely fine art to deliver criticism – even intentionally constructive criticism – in a way that helps the recipient improve upon the work they have done, or the understanding they have, without any negative impact upon that individual's outlook. Rather than risking the demotivating effect of poorly delivered criticism, try to encourage them in a way that isn't patronizing, complimenting them on their efforts to date, and offering new avenues to further their work in a positive manner.

Become More Modest

Just as you should look to encourage others rather than level criticism, you must learn to be open to constructive criticism yourself. By leaving your ego at the door, by learning to listen first before passing on your fount of knowledge, you will allow yourself to hear what others have to say, regardless from whom the criticism comes, even if it is someone you perceive as less experienced than yourself. Just as we need to bring many perspectives to the table at the earliest possible time in the SDLC to create a more complete picture, the perspectives of others, whether complete novices in comparison to yourself and your area of expertise, or someone you hold in high regard, their input into how you can improve can be invaluable.

Never attempt to shut down someone trying to provide this kind of feedback, even if you think it is just plain wrong. Take the time to step back and thoroughly examine what they have said, and why they have brought it up. Even if there is no perceived intrinsic value in terms of being able to learn from their comments yourself, they will provide some valuable insight into their thoughts and what it may be that they need to help them increase their knowledge, or improve their interactions and communication within the team.

Become More Empathetic

Working in a team with other individuals will always create some level of conflict in one form or another; it's part of the group dynamic. When you do have a difference of opinion with a colleague, be mindful of arguing your case aggressively, and remember the advice of leaving your ego at the door. If you're intent on arguing the case as you feel that you have the right answer, you can come across like a dog with a bone, and this aggressive stance can quickly become a slippery slope that leads to an erosion of trust between you and your colleagues.

Try to take a step back and attempt to see things from their perspective. Think about why they believe that they are right with their opinion. If you find it difficult to metaphorically place yourself in their shoes, ask them why they believe what they do, and do a little digging to uncover the reasoning behind that belief. You will gain a better understanding of your colleague and their motivations, and who knows, you may even discover some useful information that you were missing that may influence your own opinion that you were so eager to push for in the first place.

Become More Positive

This can be easier said than done. It's not going to be possible to be positive 100 percent of the time, and that's not what we're aiming for. All we're looking to do is to adjust your usual disposition to be slightly more upbeat than usual. Being positive fosters a better working atmosphere for both you and your colleagues, and it has a tremendous effect on how others work with you as a result.

I was once told a story about the two different types of people that you will find in our working environments. The concept around which these two types of people revolved was joy. One type were the joy givers, the ones who were upbeat, confident in the job they were doing, and seemed to revel in how that would make a positive impact on those around them, creating a self-fulfilling cycle of positivity. On the other hand were the joy suckers: those who wallowed in their negative attitude, draining the joy out of those around them, and creating a negative atmosphere around them, infecting their colleagues with pessimism. I have found myself in both of those camps at many different points throughout my career, and I can tell you, it's far better to be a giver than a sucker.

Listen to Others

In becoming more modest, we briefly mentioned how we should learn to listen before speaking. There is quite a difference between listening to reply, and listening to understand. A study carried out by Charles G. Gross at Princeton University in June 2010 found that there is a lag between what you hear and what you understand, and that lag can vary by individual from a few seconds up to a minute. Within that period of lag, we start to listen to ourselves and not the other person, leading to a drop-off in our levels of comprehension.

To begin to listen better, you need to become more passive. Take the time to listen to others, to hear them out with their ideas and suggestions. If you can avoid shutting down ideas at the earliest possible opportunity and hear your colleagues out, it makes them feel like their opinion and input is valued, which in turn makes them feel valued as part of the team, and benefits you by increasing your comprehension on the subject of the discussion. This, along with all of the other principles we have gone through, really helps to improve the perception of yourself as part of the team, and goes quite some way to breaking the stereotypes developers who can be seen as stubborn and arrogant.

Believe it or not, anyone can have a great idea; you never know where the next one will come from.

Provide Clarity

Last, but most definitely not least, is providing clarity. All of your communication, be it verbal, written, or even as comments throughout your code, must provide a level of clarity that can be understood by all of your fellow team members. Always bear in mind the cognitive bias that comes in the form of the "curse of knowledge." It is extremely easy to fall into the trap of communicating with others while assuming that those people have the background or knowledge to fully understand what you are trying to communicate. Never be afraid to ask, "is that clear?" after you have been conversing with your team. Not only is there no harm in making sure that everyone is on the same page and holds the same understanding of a particular topic, it goes a great deal of the way to removing any future misunderstandings around the project you are working on.

Improving Designer/Developer Relationships

If you work as a developer in an Agile environment, you may be familiar with the concept of pair programming. Essentially, two developers will work together at the same workstation. There are two roles that the developers adopt in this scenario; the 'driver' writes the code, while the 'observer' reviews the code as it is written. This allows both developers to build an understanding between them, create a common way of working, to share knowledge, and improve communication. These roles would be switched frequently, and over time the developers would adjust their habits in such a way that they will both write their code in the same way, making it easier for the rest of the development team to pick up.

By adapting this approach and replacing one of the developers with the designer, we can create a designer-developer pairing that allows both roles to be in constant communication with each other. And just as we would reverse the driver and observer roles when pair programming, we can switch the roles in designer-developer pairing in relation to the design and implementation phases of the SDLC.

While in the design phase, the designer would be the driver as they work through creating the journeys and interfaces that the developer would eventually implement, while the developer would take on the role of observer, offering guidance and technical advice on the art of the possible.

On moving to the implementation phase, the roles would switch. The developer would become the driver, and the designer the observer. Through my own personal experience as a developer working in this fashion, I have found that this is an approach that lends itself perfectly to the process of building out the front end of responsive websites. By sitting next to each other, working side by side throughout the course of a project, I was able to fire questions at the designer about the intentions of each component on the screen, how they intended them to react as the size of the viewport changed, how they would behave alongside other components, and many other things that you should consider with a responsive website build.

For me, this more casual approach to the pairing between developer and designer worked well in this particular scenario, but for larger teams with a wider range of priorities, more concentrated pairing sessions can be used to condense the transfer of knowledge in a shorter period. While this can be quite intense compared to an ongoing conversation that is picked up as and when needed, both are viable approaches depending on what best fits your working situations.

Ultimately, after employing this technique at different intensities on many varying responsive website projects, the designer-developer pairing approach helped us to streamline both the design and development workflows. Firstly, we came to the realization that we could reduce the work a designer had to do for the multiple layouts at different breakpoints for a responsive design. Rather than creating three or four (or sometimes even more) designs at popular device resolutions, the designer would produce two sets of designs: one for the smallest screen, and one for the largest. As a proponent of the mobile-first approach, I would build out the designs for the smallest screen first, and then begin to build on this layout as the available viewport size increased. Always with one eye on how the design would look at the largest screen sizes, I would be in constant conversation with the designer as things would look broken as they reached larger sizes. Wherever a component seemed to break down at a certain size, we would work together, adjusting the layout accordingly, and creating breakpoints based on the components in the design, rather than on the rather arbitrary viewport sizes of particular mobiles, tablets, laptops, or desktop machines.

As you can probably imagine, by working like this, both the developer and the designer gain a great insight into the many facets of each other's roles. The constant availability of each other to ask questions, quell doubts, and to have answers freely provided without fear of being made to feel inferior, creates one of the most prolific partnerships in terms of both productivity and growth. At the very least, the designer learns a little about development, and the developer learns a little about design. At most, a designer and developer working hand in hand like this can be the catalyst to creating truly great user experiences, while creating a shared understanding of each other's roles. This shared understanding can become the first steps into the world of user experience for the developer, creating empathy with their designer; and by extension of their work, the start of gaining empathy for the user.

Breaking Down Barriers

Working together in a designer-developer pairing, or closely with other members of your team is a noble goal, but there can be many barriers that can hamper this kind of collaborative working.

If you're looking to utilize a designer-developer pairing to improve the communication and day-to-day working relationships between these two disciplines, physical location can become an issue. With remote working becoming more prevalent in many organizations, it can be very difficult to get the required amount of time working collaboratively in this manner to reap the benefits. The more time you can work in close communication with your team, the greater the benefits you will be able to enjoy.

Although it can be customary for developers to shut themselves away to get into the zone when coding, it is helpful to the other members of the team that you are able to make yourself available when needed. After all, if you become someone who is seen as unapproachable, or if you hide behind the distances that may separate you physically, all of your efforts to become a more valuable member of the team will go to waste. There is a careful balancing act that you must master with this in order to give yourself the space and time to get your head down, lock yourself away from distractions, and get stuck into some serious coding sessions. This is another skill that that takes time and experience to master.

Try different ways of breaking down your time into manageable chunks; create a continuous block of time if you need to spend time getting in the zone, and allow time around that to stay up to date on emails, instant messaging, and to communicate with your team.

If you need to lock yourself away, prepare your colleagues for what that entails. Provide the clarity to your colleagues as to why this may be necessary, but remember to listen to their concerns, and try to be more empathetic with their predicament. Notify everyone beforehand that you have set a block of time aside to simply get work done; not many will begrudge you doing what you are paid to do. Take care of your constant stream of emails by setting an auto-responder stating that you're unavailable, but you will check your email at predefined times during the day, so people can know when to expect an answer. Framing this approach in a positive light will give you the time and space you need to work, without creating barriers between you and your team.

Understanding the Needs of Your Team

Outside of Silicon Valley and similar conglomerates of tech-focused companies, there are relatively few developers who "get" design, and a similar number of designers who "get" development. An individual's understanding of these seemingly contrasting disciplines varies according to their level of exposure to it. I had worked for almost a decade as a web developer before I had even begun to take any kind of interest in the design process.

I, like many of the developers I have worked with over the years, had a very analytical and logical approach to the work we did. That analytical mind-set is a fundamental underpinning to becoming a good developer or software engineer. The analytical mind can be seen to be at odds with the creative mind associated with designers, and this can be apparent when conflicts between designers and developers arise. There can be varied and numerous reasons for this conflict. One particular example I have encountered myself on multiple occasions is that an underlying system simply prohibits a particular feature within a design, or prevents an ideal user journey from being plausible. As a designer it is impossible to design for these kinds of situations without the knowledge that this kind of constraint exists. This doesn't only affect the designers, but the team as a whole.

The team, as a whole, should function as a team should, as a single organism looking to achieve a common goal. To become a successful team, the skills of the individual must complement those of their colleagues, essentially creating a dynamic that is greater than the sum of its parts. The skills and knowledge you bring to the team as a developer – or as any other member of that team – inform and guide the thoughts and decisions of your colleagues, providing a more rounded understanding from multiple perspectives and disciplines.

Put Your Ego to One Side

Something that will starve a team of its success is for the individual within the team to be insular, to be selfish, and to withhold their knowledge that they may see as proprietary: something that they earned through hard work, so why should they freely share this?

One of the key traits that you will need to eradicate from your own personality to become a developer who is an integral part of the team, a developer who puts the needs of the user first and foremost, is your ego.

This trait is not just confined to the role of the developer and can be found in any individual as egos are fed by external factors as well as a conceited view of your own knowledge and ability.

The only way to reduce the influence of your ego on your behavior is to begin employing the six guiding principles for better communication that we covered earlier in this chapter. Over time, encouraging others, being more modest, empathetic, and positive, the realization will occur that you are a more valuable member of the team when your goals align with those of the team.

The Curse of Knowledge: Assumptions and the Obvious

Although keeping your own ego in check is something that will help the team overall, it does not lessen the beneficial impact that your knowledge will have, nor the skills that you bring to the team.

It is not easy for us to always consider the fact that not everyone knows what we know. It is a natural process (or lack thereof) of human thought to assume that the knowledge you have already resides inside the minds of others. This is a cognitive bias referred to as the curse of knowledge. It occurs when you are communicating with other individuals, and you unknowingly assume that the others already have the same level of knowledge around the subject matter that you do.

Unlike the ability to maintain a flexible perspective between that of a developer and that of a user as we covered in the previous section, this is more relevant to your product team and other colleagues within your organization. You have to be consciously aware that others will not share the same knowledge that you have gained through your years of experience in your role, or through your time in a particular organization.

Have you ever taken a look back at some of your old work? Something from a year ago, or perhaps just a month or two back? You spot functions and classes that make you wonder what the hell you were thinking as you wrote it. You see CSS rules and DOM structures that look bloated and outdated. You can think of a dozen different ways you could make this better off the top of your head right now. The reason this happens is because you have the benefit of hindsight coupled with advances in your own knowledge. Now think of when you last took a look at someone else's code. Same thing happened, right?

You are looking at this work – whether your own or someone else – through your own lens of experience of knowledge. One that warps your perspective and makes you ask questions like "Why didn't they just do it this way?," or "Why didn't they follow best practice?" These kinds of questions are ultimately pointless. What we do need to understand are the decisions that were made, and the reasons behind them: the "why" behind the work.

Communication is once again key. The collective knowledge of the team will allow you to uncover the underlying factors that would have led to the completed solution, along with another form of communication: documentation.

Beyond Verbal Communication

Documentation is a staple form of communication in the world of software development and user experience design. Modern development methodologies – such as Agile – can lead to the thought that less documentation is better, that it "trims the fat" and allows you to put your time and effort into the "real work." This is rarely the case. Documentation is something that is often valued in consumption and despised in creation. And yet the value of documentation cannot be realized without its creation in the first place. I'm sure there are others out there like me who don't really enjoy the documentation, but it forms an integral part of the deliverables of any project, of any code base.

You will not always be working on the same project, or you may move to another team or to another organization. You may work in remote teams across time zones, or your project may be put on hold only for it to be restarted a year later. In all of these scenarios, the benefit of documentation is obvious, not only to yourself, but to anyone else who may to work some on the product in the future. It is a valuable record of progress, decisions, and direction: one that can help to form the basis of a common understanding.

One thing that would be wise to remember is that documentation alone does not constitute communication. It is an aid to communication. The act of sending an email with a set of documents and leaving the recipient to go away, read everything, and to come to the same shared understanding that you have is not communication. It is not your job to provide information in this manner, but it is part of your job to make your colleagues understand the things that you have created. Be mindful that documentation is ideal for reference and clarification, but it does not replace the need for direct communication between people.

Summary

In this chapter we have looked at the value of communication, more focused upon you and your team and organization, rather than between you and the user. The ability to communicate effectively within the teams in which you work facilitates a better understanding between each other, helping to ensure that you are all working toward the same goals and creating a better experience for your users. The guiding principles within this chapter will help to guide you in breaking down any silos that may exist across your team or organization, and is not something that will happen without applying yourself and implementing these principles. Better communication drives a more complete understanding between you and your team, what you are working together to build, and it is a foundational aspect of a successful team.

CHAPTER 6

Focusing on the User

Throughout my years as a front-end developer, my thoughts while building out websites and applications for the web revolved around delivering a consistent and functional interface. More specifically, it was about how I would create that consistency in one of, if not, the most inhospitable environments in the digital world: the web browser.

The pace at which technologies evolve when it comes to creating things on the web is truly astonishing, and this only adds more pressure on developers to keep up with new frameworks, techniques, and ways of working. But is this really where the value in the work of a developer lies? In the knowledge of the most bleeding edge advances in development? I would argue not.

Where a developer's real value lies is not only in their ability to bring products and ideas to life in a digital world, but to make them to improve the lives of other human beings. It is not the means by which something is built that makes a successful and usable product, it is the implementation that fulfills a need for real people.

While the concerns of a developer may be in the types of methodologies they adopt in their day-to-day work, it is far from the thoughts of your users, just as it may have been that your users may have been far from your own thoughts. As developers, you find yourselves at the final stages of creation of a user experience, and with that comes the power and responsibility of delivering a better user experience by applying your knowledge and skills applied to this end.

You Are Not Your User

One of the key lessons that you must learn when working on a development project, in any capacity, is that you are not your user. By definition, you cannot be a representative example of your user base as you have one key distinguishing attribute: that you are privy to the internal workings of the product.

By simply working on the product – even one that you may consider yourself a user of – you acquire the curse of knowledge, a cognitive bias that an individual unknowingly assumes that others have the background to adopt the same level of understanding. It can be difficult to remove yourself from your own frame of reference, to recognize this curse of knowledge when designing and developing a product for someone other than yourself.

As well as the curse of knowledge, there is another cognitive bias that can affect the whole team working on a development project. The false-consensus effect is a psychological tendency where an individual will overestimate the extent to which other people's opinions, beliefs, motivations – essentially the way they think – mirror their own. This bias can lead to a consensus that may be agreed upon within your team or organization, but it does not reflect the understanding of those outside the organization: your users, for example. Thus, a false consensus is created.

Although these cognitive biases affect all human beings, their effect on developers of a project can be viewed as directly proportional to the degrees of separation from the user; the further from contact with the user you are, the greater the dissonance between their own understanding and that of the user.

The Road to Hell Is Paved with Good Intentions

To illustrate the kind of impact that good intentions that lack any grounding in empathy with the user can have, we'll work through a scenario I have encountered in the past as a user.

A few years ago, I applied for a credit card. Having amassed a number of credit cards previously, with varying levels of accumulated debt from my days as a student, I was looking to transfer the balances from my current credit cards onto a single credit card with a better interest rate. Upon finding a suitable credit card provider, I proceeded with the application online. This particular credit card would allow me to transfer multiple balances to the new card at the point of application.

Unfortunately, upon completion of the form, and once a credit check was carried out behind the scenes, I was not offered a card with a sufficient credit limit that would allow me to transfer all of my other debts on to this single card. It was then that something akin to Figure 6-1 was presented to me.

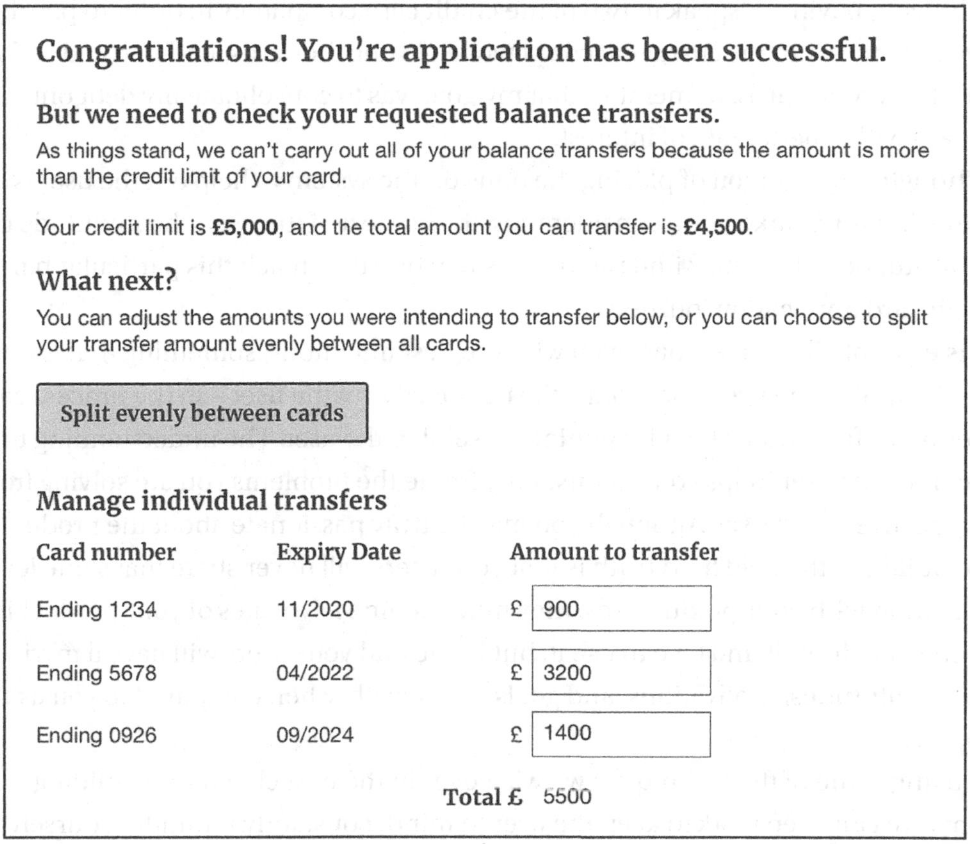

> ## Congratulations! You're application has been successful.
>
> ### But we need to check your requested balance transfers.
>
> As things stand, we can't carry out all of your balance transfers because the amount is more than the credit limit of your card.
>
> Your credit limit is **£5,000**, and the total amount you can transfer is **£4,500**.
>
> ### What next?
>
> You can adjust the amounts you were intending to transfer below, or you can choose to split your transfer amount evenly between all cards.
>
> [**Split evenly between cards**]
>
> ### Manage individual transfers
>
> | Card number | Expiry Date | Amount to transfer |
> |---|---|---|
> | Ending 1234 | 11/2020 | £ 900 |
> | Ending 5678 | 04/2022 | £ 3200 |
> | Ending 0926 | 09/2024 | £ 1400 |
> | | **Total £** | 5500 |

Figure 6-1. *Example interface highlighting a solution that is not user focused*

At first glance, this screen is something I would expect to see in order to help me, as a user, to transfer the right amounts from the other cards I own on to the one I am applying for. At first glance it looks like there's also a magic button that will solve the new problem that I have now: that I don't have a sufficient credit limit.

On closer inspection, the purpose of this button is to evenly distribute the available credit limit evenly across the cards I wish to transfer my balances from. The total amount that can be transferred to the new card is £4,500. If I were to click this button, the function would attempt to take £1,500 from the three cards to fill the available credit limit of £4,500. Functionally, this is a sound premise, but in a real-life scenario, it can raise more problems than it solves.

In this particular example, using this function will result in two of the three cards having a positive balance, while the remaining card would still have a remaining balance of £1,700. As a user, this is not what I want at all. In fact, it would actually make my life more difficult, having to speak to two of the credit card companies in order to pay the positive balances into my current account while closing the cards, and it would still leave me with two credit cards. Remember that my goal was to consolidate my debt onto a single card with a better rate of interest.

Although the intention of placing the onus on the system to help out the user is a good one, it has not taken into consideration the context of the user: the multitude of different situations they may find themselves in when they reach this particular part of the credit card application journey.

This example illustrates that, even with the best intentions, something that is built without including the user – or at least the perspective of the user – in the process can be poles apart from that which is genuinely useful to the user. The understanding that you are not your user helps you to constantly frame the problems you are solving from the perspective of the user. Although you may be truly passionate about the product you are building, the cold hard truth is that your users will never share that same level of connection with your product. Yes, they may become advocates of your product if they gain value from it and love to use it, but in the end your users will have a myriad of different attitudes, motivations, and goals – especially when compared to you as the developer.

By using some of the techniques we will cover in the next chapter on building empathy, we can keep work to keep the user in mind, constantly reminding ourselves that their needs and goals are very different to that of the developer.

Reducing Cognitive Load

Cognitive load is a term that refers to the amount of effort being used in the working memory of an individual. Working memory is the cognitive system that is utilized for temporarily holding information while we process it, and it has a limited capacity. Think of working memory as RAM in a computer; it is where a computer stores the data that it is actively using for the task at hand.

By reducing the number of items that a user has to think about while attempting to complete a task, we can effectively reduce the cognitive load for an individual, meaning that the user's brain will not have to work as hard to complete that task. Essentially, providing less choice enables the user to quickly make decisions and move through a process more efficiently, which in itself is rewarding to the user.

The Myth of Miller's Number

It is often thought that the working memory can hold seven, plus or minus two items, for processing. Unfortunately, what has become known as "Miller's Number" is a myth due to the misinterpretation of a research paper published by the cognitive psychologist George A. Miller back in 1956.

The magic number of 7±2 has been commonly, and incorrectly, used as a guideline for determining the number of items that should be presented to a user at a single time, oftentimes referring to the number of items that should reside in the navigation menu of a website or application.

In a digital interface, the user will rarely commit the available options to memory in order to make a decision, as they are generally visually present. It's more important to keep these options visible and accessible to the user at all times so that we are not making them do more thinking than they need to. Rather than utilizing methods to hide and show content within an interface, or hide navigation behind a button on smaller screens, think about what makes it easier for a user to get around your website or application, and not to place the interesting and cool things that you could build as a higher priority.

The Truth of Hick's Law

Although Miller's Number has been misappropriated, there are alternative psychological findings that do support the need to reduce cognitive load for our users, the most well-known being Hick's Law.

Also known as the Hick-Hyman Law, named after the psychologists William Edmund Hick and Ray Hyman, Hick's Law, as depicted in Figure 6-2, is defined as the following: the time it takes to make a decision increase proportionally to the number and complexity of choices.

It can be conveyed in the following equation:

$$RT = a + b \log2 (n)$$

RT is the Reaction Time, n is the number of stimuli, and a and b are measurable constants that depend on the task and the conditions under which the task will be carried out.

For anyone like me who is terrible at understanding mathematical formulas such as this, we can plot this on a graph to depict the effect that an increasing number of choices has for a user with regard to time spent making a decision.

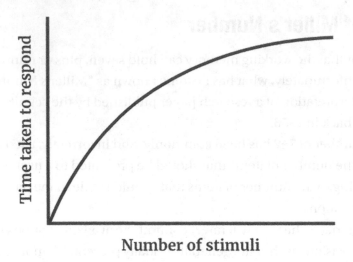

Figure 6-2. *A depiction of Hick's Law*

The application of the law in relation to user experience is rather straightforward: reduce the number of stimuli, thereby creating an environment for faster decision making. The more straightforward and simpler something is to use, the faster the user can reach their goal. Again, we are looking to avoid introducing overly complex interactions between the user and the interface; we should look to avoid overloading them with visual information and cues that can distract them from the tasks they wish to complete.

Deriving Simplicity from Complexity

Simplicity, by definition, is the absence of complexity. Complexity is often understood to mean something that is hard to understand, but it can also be defined as something with many interconnected parts. Therefore, it is possible that simplicity and complexity are not mutually exclusive. Something can be both simple to use and complex in nature by having many interconnected parts.

When we contemplate what consists a good user experience, one of the prevailing characteristics is simplicity; ease of use. When a person finds something easy to use, it will be perceived as though it were simple and straightforward. If a user experience works as it was intended – as it was designed – the user will not notice any of the work that went into it and would more likely comment on how easy it was to use when compared to some of their previous experiences when trying to complete a similar journey or task elsewhere.

To become a developer that values the user experience, there must be a realization that the work you do is, first and foremost, intended to benefit the human beings who use what you make. Oftentimes this results in more work for us in order to create less work for our users. This is a key aspect to delivering truly user-focused experiences, and one we must become accustomed to as we look to adjust our attitude to the work we do and who it is for.

With the knowledge that we as developers have with regard to the system, the underlying processes of the digital products we build, we must be the ones to implement the user interfaces through which our users – those who do not share our level of knowledge – will engage with our product.

As we look to shield our users from the complexity of the underlying technology that we are familiar with, and work with every day, we must recognize the methods that we can employ to reduce complexity for our users to deliver a simple, usable product. We'll now take a look through a number of design-led approaches that will help us to understand the ways in which we can look to implement a more intuitive way of interacting with an otherwise complex system.

Minimizing Choice

In line with Hick's Law, the reduction of stimuli on a page helps the user to make decisions more quickly. It is quite easy to imagine a minimal layout, with only a small number of possible choices for the user to make, guiding them down predetermined paths that will help them to achieve their goals.

However, we must tread carefully when it comes to minimalism. An oft-repeated quote can be heard when designers point toward a minimalist approach.

> *"Perfection is achieved, not when there is nothing more to add, but when there is nothing left to take away."*
>
> —Antoine de Saint-Exupéry, French writer (1900 – 1944)

While this ideology seems commendable, by no means is minimalism the design direction that should always be employed to solve every issue surrounding the reduction of complexity. Minimalism does not necessarily equate to simplicity.

It is quite easy to focus on the removal of features and functionality, to visually hide the complex to such an extent that it becomes even harder for a user to comprehend what steps to take next, even when compared to having all of the possible functionality visible at once. There is always a balance to be found between the number of stimuli presented to the user and the reduction of complexity, and it is by researching and observing your users that will help you to strike this balance.

This approach to minimizing choice is often seen as the path to reducing complexity to the user and making your product easier to use. The Google home page, an example of which is shown in Figure 6-3, is often held as a shining example of simplicity. A single search term input is the focus for the user in the center of the screen, creating a single task for the user to complete their goal; type in the thing you are looking for.

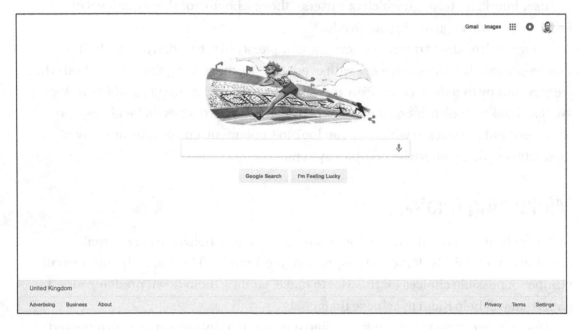

Figure 6-3. *A screenshot of the Google home page*

Google, as an example of simplicity, is often held in comparison to sites such as Yahoo! and MSN. Although many may think of all three of these websites as search engines, MSN and Yahoo!, as depicted in Figures 6-4 and 6-5 respectively, are actually web directories, packed with information and links rather than just behaving as a search engine, making it more like comparing apples and oranges.

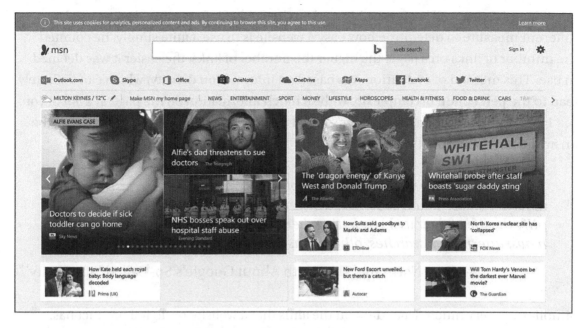

Figure 6-4. *A screenshot of the MSN home page*

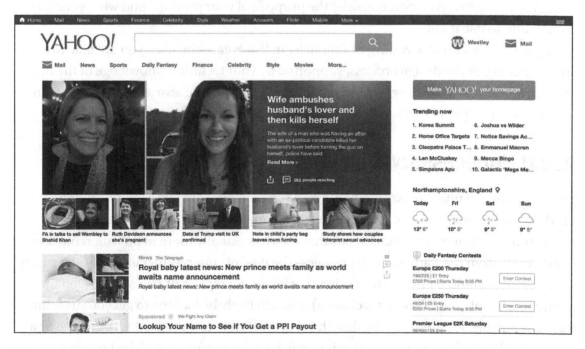

Figure 6-5. *A screenshot of the Yahoo home page*

Edward Tufte, well known for his work in the field of information design, used a different measure to determine how easy a website is to use. Quite simply, he counted the number of links on a page; the higher the number of links, the easier it was deemed to use. This method of evaluation was based on information density, which can definitely lead to the perception of complexity with so much information on the page in front of you.

Don Norman suggests that a user's initial perception of complexity may actually be an artifact of the product's simplicity.

> *"Why are Yahoo! and MSN such complex-looking places? Because their systems are easier to use. Not because they are complex, but because they simplify the life of their users by letting them see their choices on the home page: news, alternative searches, other items of interest."*
>
> —Don Norman, "The Truth About Google's So-Called 'Simplicity'"

Simplicity is very much dependant on the aims that a website or digital product has. Although minimizing choice is a good way to avoid cognitive overload of the people using your product, you must consider the purpose of your product, and what your users are looking to use it for.

By gaining an understanding of simplicity in the eyes of the user, you are able to lend your expertise to the design process, supported by your technical knowledge of the most feasible solutions. In keeping the same frame of mind, you are also able to temper your own ideas for implementation, putting simplicity ahead of technical achievement.

Avoid Unnecessary Elements

The avoidance of unnecessary elements on a screen may seem like a simplification of minimizing choice – some of you may feel that something like the Yahoo! home page has a large amount of superfluous information – it is actually more to do with removing distractions from the path of the user. Unless the goal of your product is to sell advertising space like an online billboard (that brings back fond memories of The Million Dollar Home Page; look it up if you get a chance), you will likely be looking to get your user into the right journey for them to complete the task they came to your product for in the first place, which will also fulfill a measurable goal from the perspective of the business.

A classic example of where the removal of unnecessary elements comes into play is in "the funnel." This may be a multistep form, a newsletter sign-up form, or an e-commerce checkout; essentially it is a predefined journey that we are looking for our users to complete, while maintaining as high a conversion rate as possible to meet the goals of the business. If we were to place flashing banner advertisements throughout an e-commerce checkout process, we vastly increase the risk of a user becoming distracted from their task at hand, leading to users abandoning their journey. That is neither good for the user nor the business.

By removing unnecessary distractions, we reduce the probability of a user abandoning their task. If we were more concerned with form over utility, we will often find our resulting journeys and experiences to lack direction, providing no clear signposts as to what the user should do next, leaving them stranded in a confusing and frustrating situation.

Form follows function is a principle that says the shape of an object should primarily relate to its intended function or purpose. This is not something that should be adhered to in a fundamentalist fashion, but as a guideline to keep in mind that the function that a particular feature offers to the user is there to help them achieve their goal. Always be mindful that adding clutter and distraction to this kind of functionality will likely dilute its effectiveness, both for the user and for the business.

Make the System Do the Work

As we have covered earlier in this book, in order to realign your thinking to make the user experience the focus of your work, we must be willing to apply the extra effort to take the complex nature of our internal systems away from our users and present them with more usable and enjoyable experiences.

By placing the onus on the system to complete the more intricate aspects of a process, it moves the complexity away from the domain of the user, leaving them with a more refined interface with which to interact. For example, let's compare the task of changing gear in a vehicle with an automatic gearbox to the same task in a vehicle with a manual gearbox.

In a vehicle with a manual gearbox, there are a number of signals the driver must process in order to make the decision as to when to change gear. They will listen to the pitch of the engine or look at the rev counter to decide when to shift up or down in a given situation on the road. Then the act of changing gearLift foot up from the accelerator.

1.   Press the clutch to the floor.

2.   Move the gear stick to the required gear.

3. Slowly lift foot up from the clutch to the biting point.

4. Let up on the clutch while pushing down on the accelerator.

In a vehicle with an automatic gearbox, there is no need to worry about changing gear. The driver can accelerate and decelerate without thinking about the point at which to shift into the right gear. An automatic gearbox takes away the complexities and cognitive load required of a driver to change gears while driving a vehicle.

The additional work required to create an internal system that, to all intents and purposes, would be hidden from the user will most definitely be seen as a great deal of additional effort for the engineers that designed and built that system. The engineers would not be the ones to benefit from their extra effort, but the resulting benefit for the users will be the yardstick by which their efforts should be measured.

Be mindful of the needs of the user when new functionality and user journeys are proposed for your digital products. It may be instinctual to have a negative reaction and to immediately put up blockers to the progress of potentially large changes to back-end systems or the front-end code base. What may seem like a disproportionate amount of development work for a seemingly small improvement to the user experience is often a moot point; you have the power and the skill as a developer to create a system that does the heavy lifting on behalf of the user, making their lives easier. It's also worth considering that making something more usable does not necessarily equate to more annoying work; it can still be both challenging and interesting to build out these solutions.

Users Are Not Stupid

If you've ever had the chance to watch a usability testing session of a digital product that you have built where the user couldn't complete the task they had started, listened to support calls from frustrated customers trying to find something on the website, or transcripts of live chats where a user could not figure out what to do next, you may have had one of two reactions. You either felt empathy with them and began thinking about how you could make your product easier for that person to use, or you had the "user is stupid" reaction.

For developers who are not exposed to real people using their creations, this can be an all-too-common reaction. It is not right to think of a user as stupid when they cannot use an interface in the way it was intended, especially when the interface does not make clear to the user what they need to do, or how they should use it. The problem will most likely be that the interface is failing to communicate what input or interaction is required to its users.

And yet I have had this reaction myself, as have colleagues of mine, you have probably had this reaction, and I have no doubt that there are other developers out there, right at this moment, who are thinking that their users are stupid. This is a common side effect of the curse of knowledge that we covered earlier in the chapter. The fact that we are so familiar with our own product and how it works – how it is designed to work – puts us at a disadvantage when trying to place ourselves in the shoes of those who will use our product without all of the knowledge we have acquired with our constant interaction with it.

Once there is a realization that the user being unable to complete a task that your product was designed to help them complete is actually down to the design of the product, you should be able to put yourself in a position to correct the problem. The reason I say should here is that there is a need to let go of the work we create as it is not something that belongs to us as the creators, but to those who use it. If we can put our egos aside, if we can learn from the mistakes we have made, we can concentrate on making our products easier to use for those without specialist knowledge of our products.

There are a couple of methods that we can use in conjunction with which we can shape our approach as developers in order to reframe our understanding of our users. The first is to familiarize yourself with the concept of Occam's Razor, a problem-solving principle that states:

When presented with competing hypothetical answers to a problem, one should select the one that makes the fewest assumptions.

Or, to paraphrase the concept:

With all things being equal, the simplest solution is the best.

The stereotypical developer will have a logical mind, one that would most likely look for the simplest solutions to the programming challenges they are facing. The benefits to developers are numerous when applying the simplest solutions to a given problem: easy-to-understand code, fewer possible points of failure, higher efficiency, simpler testing, easier maintenance, and probably many more benefits beyond these that would benefit you and your fellow developers.

But these benefits are only for the internal team, they don't necessarily provide a direct and measurable improvement to the experience of your users. By applying the same principle from a user's perspective, you will be able to create simpler interfaces and more usable functionality within your product that will generate both a better user experience and better results for the business.

However, simplification of a digital product is not only down to a more usable or simplified interface; it must also rely on the mental models that people have already built up utilizing your digital products, as well as a whole host of other applications and websites.

A mental model is a representation of how a person understands a given process in the real world. For example, let's take a look at the mental model I have when making a cup of tea.

1. Find a mug

2. Find a teaspoon

3. Find a teabag

4. Find some milk

5. Place teabag in mug

6. Fill kettle with water

7. Boil kettle

8. Pour boiling water into mug

9. Stir tea

10. Add milk

11. Remove teabag

12. Drink tea

Your mental model may differ from mine, and no doubt some of you will be having nightmares about the fact that I add milk before removing the teabag! Some of you will have an additional step of adding sugar, some of you won't add milk, and most of you will do some of the individual tasks in a different order than I would. This does not mean that the way I make tea is superior to that of anyone else; it does not make everyone who utilizes a different method stupid.

You must take the time to observe users and how they interact with your prototypes, your products, and even the products of competitors. By understanding the mental models of our users – the order in which they expect to complete tasks or receive stimulus – we can mimic what their preferred path to the completion of a particular task may be. We can provide them with their simplest solution, while taking on the interesting and challenging work that surrounds this.

Utilize Recognized Patterns

The human brain is hard-wired to recognized patterns. From seeing the silhouettes of animals in clouds as they pass overhead, to seeing faces in inanimate objects, the human brain has an uncanny ability to recognize patterns even when there are none. It is always actively seeking ways to make sense of its visual surroundings, looking for relationships between elements of input, and patterns serve to fortify these relationships.

By taking advantage of the human brain's natural propensity to uncover patterns, we are able to create design patterns that users become accustomed to, and eventually come to build an expectation as to how certain design patterns work. When design patterns are employed correctly, they can help shape a user's understanding of how a given design pattern works, reinforcing their understanding, which in turn helps them in completing their tasks and reaching their goals.

Over time, some design patterns have become so intrinsic to design on the web that they have become a self-evidently recognized truth: a design axiom. Here are a few questions about particular design axioms that can be found on the web:

1. What do you expect to happen when you click on the company logo in the top left-hand corner of a website?

2. Where do you expect to see a link to log in or register on a website?

3. Where do you expect to find a search function on a website?

4. Where do you expect to find the main navigation on a website?

Although a few of you may have some slight variations on the answers, the majority of you reading will have answered with the following:

1. Go to the home page

2. Top right

3. Top right

4. Across the top or down the left-hand side

These design patterns have been utilized by so many websites over the years that these are now expected by users. If you buck the trend without a very good reason, you risk alienating your users with elements of design that they cannot associate with the patterns they have learned over the years that they have spent browsing the web.

Moving away from axioms, we find ourselves in a realm of design patterns that can be commonly understood, despite taking a variety of different visual forms across the web. Let's take a look at some examples of how "Cards" have been implemented as a design pattern. As we can see from the following examples, depicted in Figures 6-6 through 6-8, there are many visual variations on this particular design pattern.

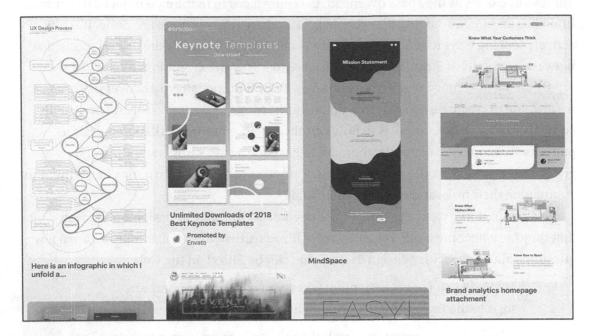

Figure 6-6. *Example of the "card" design pattern used on Pinterest*

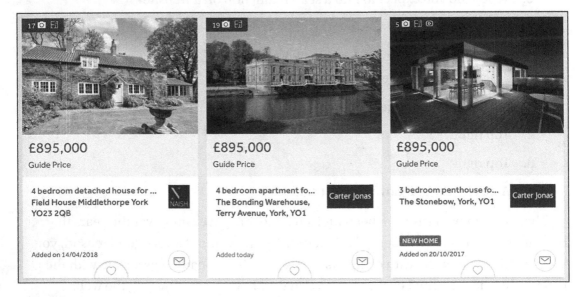

Figure 6-7. *Example of the "card" design pattern used on Rightmove*

Figure 6-8. *Example of the "card" design pattern used on the BBC website*

Despite the differing styles of visual design that overlay this particular design pattern, each of them is built upon the same underlying elements, types of content, and interaction principles; they have the same foundations, as shown in Figure 6-9.

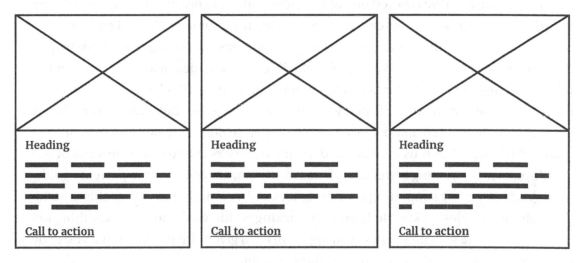

Figure 6-9. *A wireframe version of the "card" design pattern*

Over time, encountering this pattern more often across different websites, and in different contexts, creates a recurring theme, reinforcing the user's understanding of the design pattern.

Not only are these design patterns beneficial to users, but they offer the ability to remove conjecture from the work of designers and developers. By developing and testing design patterns with users, we are able to build up our own pattern libraries for our digital products.

There is – as with most things when it comes to user experience design – a balance to be struck between the use of commonly understood design patterns and the avoidance of creating a homogeneous design. Deviating from these commonly understood patterns can be done when it is meaningful to do so: when it adds value to the user and improves their experience.

As we mentioned earlier, form follows function, and these recognized design patterns are a testament to that. But the application of different aesthetics, the visual veneer that differentiates your product from the competition can be an important instrument in creating a more engaging experience for the user, despite utilizing the same patterns that you will find strewn throughout the World Wide Web.

Summary

In this chapter we have covered one of the most important lessons that has to be learned in order to deliver better user experiences: you are not your user. We looked at the working memory of the human brain, and how reducing the cognitive load can help users to achieve their goals. We dispelled the ill-conceived idea of Miller's Number in relation to digital products and created an understanding of Hick's Law that would help us to create environments for faster decision making. We also took time to work through a number of design-led approaches that will help us to create greater simplicity in our work, all of which helps us to better understand our users and to place the focus of our development on creating better experiences for them, giving you more power to guide a user experience by supporting your designers, or by centering your thoughts around your user where design knowledge may be lacking within your team. The key thing to learn is not in the specifics of how you apply this in a given situation, but that you allow it to permeate your thoughts across everything you do.

CHAPTER 7

Building Empathy

Empathy is the ability to understand and share the feelings of others, to be able to put yourself in their shoes. Empathy can easily be confused with sympathy, which is actually about feeling compassion or pity for the difficulties of another individual, but lacks the aspect of understanding the feelings of the party to which you are sympathetic.

In order to be able to empathize with someone, to share their feelings, you must either share a real connection with them or encounter the same experience. In earlier chapters, we mentioned that everyone's experiences are unique; their view of the world is filtered through their own previous experiences and needs, particular to them. Although it could be argued that the exact same experience will never be had by two different individuals, it is possible to empathize with an, albeit slightly generalized, experience that an aggregation of people – perhaps a persona – will have in relation to a product.

For a developer, as well as other members of a product team, the most reasonable and accessible approach to creating empathy with users is to go through an experience as they would, while being informed and guided by their motivations and goals. The best way in which you can generate empathy is to come into contact with real users, to create that real connection with them.

Unfortunately, it's not always possible to give all members of the team access to their users – in fact, it can be rather difficult to get any access to users at all in some cases – and business constraints tend to come in to play with regard to budgets and timescales. However, a lack of direct access to users should not prevent us from trying to generate that empathy with our users. There are a number of tools and techniques that user experience designers have at their disposal that can help reduce the gulf that can exist between the developer and the user.

Although you, as a developer, may not be the one to organize and conduct these methods of user research and analysis, it is important that you understand what they are, how they are conducted, and how you can utilize their outcomes in your own role.

© Westley Knight 2019
W. Knight, *UX for Developers*, https://doi.org/10.1007/978-1-4842-4227-8_7

User Research

User research is the foundation on which any user experience is built. Without it, everything that follows is created without the knowledge of our users, their needs, or their goals. To do this is to build your castle on shifting sands, never truly knowing what you should be aiming to achieve, or how to satisfy your user's needs.

User research consists of a number of different techniques that can be used to learn more about your users: contextual inquiry, focus groups, individual interviews, card sorting, task analysis, and more. Each of these methods can be used at varying stages of the software development life cycle (SDLC), but all of them contribute toward you getting to understand your users. Let's take a little look into what is involved with each of these research methods.

Contextual Inquiry

This is perhaps one of the most beneficial techniques that can be employed in an attempt to truly understand your users. Users are simply observed and interviewed in their natural context, while completing their tasks with as little interference as is possible.

For example, you may be looking to discover how a number of different people with the same needs shop on an e-commerce site while in the comfort of their own home. Their task may be to find an outfit to wear to a party for the weekend, and they would go about this task as they would do on any typical day.

Because of the lack of formal setting, and with the interviewee being in the control of how to complete their task, the user is far more at ease in familiar surroundings, with a task that they would usually attempt to complete in this setting. With the exception of the interviewer occasionally interrupting to ask questions when most feasible (so as to not distract the user from the task), the contextual interview provides the most "real-life" version of events, actions, and reactions as the user works through their task to completion.

The outcome of contextual inquiries tends to be a vast amount of data that requires analysis: for example, this could be in the form of Affinity Mapping or Task Analysis.

As a developer, it will be very unlikely that you will participate directly in contextual inquiries, unless you work within an organization that has attained a very high level of UX maturity. However, if you have had researchers conducting this type of research with your users, you can be sure that the resulting findings and recommendations will be based on insight that does not just consider how users interact with your product, or your competitors' products, but how it fits into their lives, as part of their everyday living. From this, you can be certain that the needs you are satisfying for your users are real, and the work you will do as a result will aim to fulfill those needs.

Focus Groups

Focus groups consist of a number of individuals, usually between 5 and 10, where the participants are encouraged to discuss their expectations and experiences around a predetermined set of topics. A moderator leads the discussion and steers the conversations using open-ended questions, with the aim of learning more about users' attitudes and reactions to proposed concepts.

There can be a downside to this approach – in comparison to contextual inquiry or usability testing – is that you only get to hear about people's experiences secondhand; you are unable to observe the experiences being shared and cannot effectively verify what is being said. Unfortunately, what people say they do and what they actually do can be very different indeed.

Any findings from focus groups may be used to make more strategic decisions about the digital products that you work on and will rarely have a direct impact on your day-to-day work. They may conflict with findings from directly observable research techniques, such as contextual inquiry or usability testing, or what you may find in your analytics and recorded visitor sessions within your product.

Individual Interviews

As the name suggests, individual interviews focus on one person at a time. They consist of a set of questions and interview protocols that the interviewer will follow in order to uncover the information pertinent to the user, within the context of the project. One of the main advantages that individual interviews have over focus groups is that group dynamics do not play a part in conclusions you are able to draw from the activity.

As a qualitative example of user research, individual interviews offer the interviewer the opportunity to spend more time discussing topics in detail, providing a deeper understanding of the user and their needs, goals, and motivations.

Although this approach does not provide as much value for the researcher and the understanding of how users interact with your products, the insights gained can have a direct impact on what you should be working on as a matter of priority for your product. Your direct participation is not required, but the outcomes will need your input at the point at which any of the findings become part of your product backlog.

Card Sorting

Card sorting is an exercise that asks participants to organize topics into categories that make sense to them. You will need to understand your users' needs, goals, and expectations, and your own content before carrying out a card sorting session.

The exercise itself provides the opportunity for you to understand how your users expect to find certain information or functionality within a website or application. Essentially this helps you to build information architecture for your product that users will understand and perhaps already feel familiar.

As an exercise, it is actually quite revealing to participate in an internal version of card sorting. If you were to take your internal understanding of what you believe to be important to your users, and compare that with the outcomes of the card sorting carried out with your users, you can uncover the discrepancies between your understanding of what your users want and need, and what you think they do. As a mental aid, this helps you to switch your focus to your users' real needs, rather than those which may have previously been assumed or based on old evidence.

Task Analysis

JoAnn Hackos and Janice Redish wrote about task analysis in their 1998 book *User and Task Analysis for Interface Design* (John Wiley & Sons) and how it helps you to understand:

- The goals of the user: what they are looking to achieve
- The steps users take to achieve those goals
- The users' personal, social, and cultural experiences that they bring with them
- How their physical environment impacts on their ability to perform a task

A common deliverable that results from task analysis is a diagram representing the steps a user takes to complete the tasks required. These flow diagrams then help to identify areas where users may need additional help, or to eradicate unnecessary steps in the process to improve efficiency for the user in completing their task.

An understanding of how a user expects to go about completing their task – their mental model – helps you to understand the mind-set of your user. These findings can be used as a comparison against your proposed or current online journeys to see how they measure up to a user's expectations, and can even be married up with analytics data to corroborate or negate your current understanding. In some cases, for example, these findings can uncover why some aspects of your online journeys may have lower than expected conversion rates, or higher dropout percentages, and can give you directly actionable data to improve your product and your user's experience as a result.

Building Upon the Foundations of User Research

With the data gathered from research around user needs for the discoveries made to become of any use, the findings must be synthesized and converted into more concrete, more usable guidelines that will instruct the design and development phases. Ultimately, we will be looking to derive a functional specification from the combination of synthesized research findings and the objectives of the business.

The way in which this can be done is by creating an empathy map for our apparent user segments, developing a set of personas from these empathy maps, and to utilize the personas to generate the user stories that form the foundation of our functional specification (Figure 7-1).

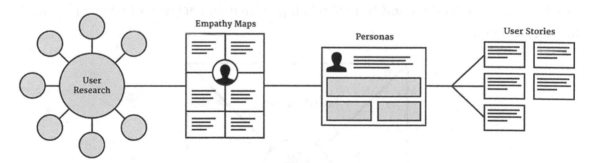

Figure 7-1. *The flow of synthesis from initial user research through empathy mapping and persona generation, culminating in a set of user stories for use in an agile-driven project*

Each of these methods helps not only designers, but the whole of the team to create a deeper understanding of their users, and what they need from a product in order for it to be something they would use to help them achieve their goals. Although developers may not be directly involved in the creation of any of these foundational pieces of documentation, there is no doubting the effect that they will have on what you work on. We'll take a look at the stages following on from the user research, how these will affect your work as a developer, and what effect you will be able to have upon them.

Empathy Mapping

One of the first steps in synthesizing the data obtained from user research is to carry out empathy mapping. When you are able to create an empathy map of the various types of user that your product is for, it can be used to align the strategy of the business to their customers' needs and goals. It generates empathy, not only for the designers, but is a wonderful tool to help those who do not usually concern themselves with the user experience to build up an understanding of their users. This approach to documenting and understanding your users is not just for the benefit of the user experience team, or even just for those within the project team; it can be utilized throughout the organization so that roles within other departments – such as operations, sales, and marketing, or even C-level executives – can start to understand their users.

Traditional empathy maps contain four of the attributes that build a picture of what the user may be thinking, feeling, saying, and doing. More modern approaches to empathy mapping combine some of these elements in order to introduce additional parameters, resulting in segments title "Think & Feel," "Say & Do," "Hear," and "See" (Figure 7-2). They can also add additional insight such as "Pains" the user has in trying to achieve their objectives, and "Gains" relating to what they achieve when completing those objectives.

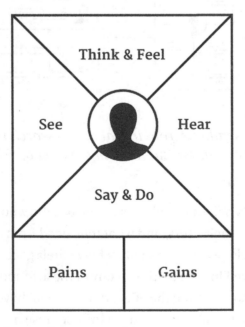

Figure 7-2. *Example of a modern empathy map canvas*

User Says

This section of the empathy map is used to record what the user says out loud during an individual interview, contextual inquiry, or some other form of usability study. These will be in the form of direct quotes, written verbatim.

User Thinks

This section is sometimes combined with the "Says" section and can contain the same content. However, this section will also include thoughts that the user may not vocalize, and this will have to be extrapolated from the raw data or exposed in follow-up questions after the study. Users may be uncomfortable externalizing some thoughts, whether they are questioning their own ability, feeling self-conscious, or just simply being polite.

User Does

This section is a record of the physical actions that the user makes throughout the period of research, considering how they interact both with the product and in the context of the setting.

User Feels

The "Feels" section is used to make notes on the user's emotional state, and how they feel about the experience as they move through their tasks.

Pains

Here we can record the difficulties a user will have while they are attempting to complete their task, as well as what foreseeable problems the user may have, and reasons for them not being able to complete their task.

Gains

Finally, under "Gains" we can record how the user came to successfully complete their task, how that success is measured by the user, and how this aligns to their larger goals.

Even if empathy mapping is not something you are exposed to, I would highly recommend seeking out a researcher or designer who may have worked on empathy maps in the past, and look to take part in a session where you work with them in order to synthesize the findings of user research into a set of empathy maps for your users. If you are able to partake in an empathy mapping session once or twice per year, you will maintain a relevant understanding of what your users think, say, and feel, along with their pain points in relation to your products, and the gains they get from using them.

Personas

A persona is a fictional personality that has been created to represent a realistic group of users for your product. These will be based on both qualitative and quantitative user research, and as a result, will provide a great deal of insight into your users without you ever having to meet them in the flesh.

There is some debate in the UX community as to the value of using personas in the design process. Some feel that personas are often created based on little or no research, meaning that they become inherently flawed in their purpose of informing the design process with regard to the users of a product. Some feel that other approaches help them to uncover user needs in a better way, utilizing frameworks like Jobs-to-be-done (JTBD).

Why Personas Are More Useful Than Jobs-to-Be-Done

First, this is not the point at which I vent my dislike at a particular approach, favoring one over the other. I have no doubt that fellow designers and UX professionals will read this and have their own differing opinions. As a developer, you may have come across both personas and jobs-to-be-done in your organization and have already made your mind up on what works or doesn't in your situation.

The reason I say that personas are more useful than JTBD is simply down to the context in which we are applying them: in this case, a developer understanding the user's motivations and goals that they are building the product to cater for.

While a persona reflects a particular segment of your users and their behaviors, the JTBD framework lifts the focus to a higher level of abstraction; rather than concentrating on the types of individuals who will be using your product and their motivations, it focuses on the "jobs" that a user "hires" your product to complete.

The JTBD framework allows those who employ the technique to worry about the outcomes rather than the features of a product. This means that JTBD functions far more effectively as a tool in the early discovery phases of a project, uncovering the high-level goals that the product should help people to achieve.

Down in the murky depths of the design and implementation phases, these overarching goals do not offer much in the way of direction for how we approach solving a particular type of problem for a particular user, in a particular scenario. As Page Laubheimer summarized his article "Personas vs. Jobs-to-Be-done" on the Nielsen Norman Group website:

> *Jobs-to-be-done focus on user problems and needs, while well-executed personas include the same information and also add behavioural and attitudinal details.*

It's those additional details, the behavioral and attitudinal aspects of the persona that give us that little bit more insight, that helps us to connect with the user, and aids in building empathy.

The Foundations of a Good Persona

First, we should understand what a good persona is. Essentially, it comes down to the persona successfully promoting empathy among the members of a product team toward their users. They serve to generate a connection between the team and who they are building their product for.

So what information do you need to create the foundations of a persona that successfully generates empathy?

Demographics

This is the staple set of information you will garner from any kind of research, regardless of the area of business to which it is applied. Demographic data is used to build a picture of your audience around common pieces of information such as age, occupation, income, marital status, nationality, and other similar attributes that can be applied to the populous at large.

Personal Information

This is a set of information that starts to create a more unique side to the persona. From demographic data and user research, it's possible to fabricate a character, providing a name, age, job title, a short biography about this individual, and even a photograph. These elements start to promote the idea that what we are building is to cater for a specific person, albeit an amalgamated personality built from qualitative and quantitative sets of data.

Attitudinal Information

This is where personas really begin to generate a level of empathy. By uncovering the feelings this persona has about the tasks they are looking to complete, their mental model about how they would expect to complete that task, and the pain points they have throughout a journey, we can really start to get under the skin of their requirements. We can dive into a real understanding of what frustrates them, what tasks they need to complete and why, and what they are expecting from a particular process or product.

Behavioral Information

Behavioral traits are more tethered to the persona and the way they conduct themselves, as opposed to the more contextual attitudinal information. For example, one of my own behavioral traits is that I tend to open new tabs in my browser for everything that I'm about to read, and leave them open so I can come back to them whenever I need (and I know some of you reading will do that, someone has even gone to the trouble of building a browser extension to manage this behavior!). Another example would be that an individual will always type and double-check their email address, rather than trusting the copy and paste function. These are elements of a persona that stick with them regardless of the context they find themselves in. Whether registering for a social media site, or submitting their tax return online, these behaviors are always present.

Motivations and Goals

These are the driving forces behind individuals' actions; the reasons why they will be using your product and what they are aiming to achieve with it. This information forms the basis of the questions that you will be looking to answer by the way in which you design and build your product.

Populating Your Personas

As we have already stated, we will require both qualitative and quantitative data in order to flesh out a persona for our product. To give a more concrete understanding of how we would build out a representation of one of our users, we will look back at the different types of user research and how we could feed those findings into a persona for our imaginary product (Figure 7-3).

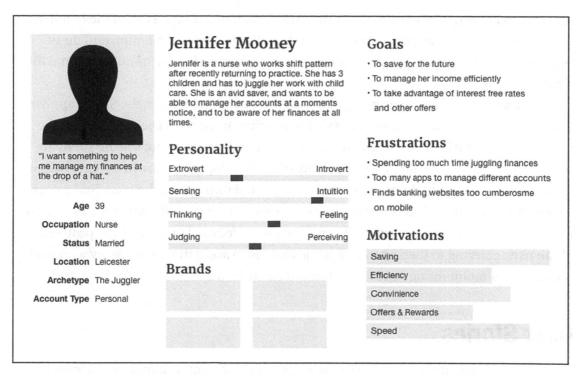

Figure 7-3. *An example of a persona*

As valuable a tool as a set of personas can be to understanding your users, they are only as good as the research upon which they are derived and a team that supports them. Personas should not be viewed as an artifact that is generated as part of the design process, but as an ever-evolving set of characters that will be with you from the design phases, through implementation, and beyond. They can evolve – just as real human beings do – over time as new details around users' motivations, behaviors, and attitudes are uncovered through continued research and analysis.

How to Utilize Personas

One of the most popular things to do with a persona – it's certainly common to everywhere I have worked – is to print them out as large posters and plaster them across the walls, making sure that they are in full view of as many people as possible. It's a nice idea; it keeps them visible, everyone who wanders past in your office can see that you have personas, ergo; you must be user-centered in your approach.

The problem with this particular approach is that it can easily make you feel like the work of the persona is done. Unfortunately, once a few weeks pass, these poster-sized personas will become part of the furniture, slowly merging into the rest of the familiar surroundings of your working environment. Familiarity breeds contempt, and these personas can easily drop out of the collective conscious, ending up as nothing more than a wall hanging.

The real value of personas comes through their continued use in the SDLC, applying them to user stories, integrating them with scenarios, and always keeping them in the minds of everyone as they work on a product. Although you may not see the surviving of a set of personas as a direct responsibility of the developer, you are in a great position to help champion them through the work you do, and throughout the team that you are constantly working and communicating with. This extra effort will contribute toward the wider understanding of your users, keeping the team focused on solving the problems of the user, catering to their needs, all while looking to avoid the unnecessary work and building and maintaining features that would rarely be used.

User Stories

If you have worked in an agile environment, you will have come across user stories. A user story is a tool used to capture the need of a user – usually related to a feature within your product – from their perspective. They are usually formatted something like this:

As an <actor>, I want to <action> so that <goal>.

They are intentionally short and written by the team working on the product, but with one very important aspect is that they *must* be written in the voice of the user. Real user stories can only be created based on research and feedback from the users. For example, let's take a look at some possible user stories for a banking app, something that you will likely use on a daily basis.

> As a current account holder, I want to quickly check my bank balance so that I can make sure I have enough money to buy the product I want.

> As a savings account holder, I want to be able to set up a standing order so that I can regularly save a set amount.

> As a business account holder, I want to be able to access my historical transactions so that I can generate accurate sales reports.

As you can see, all of these user stories are written from the point of view of a particular type of customer, each one with a particular task that they need to complete in order to accomplish their goal. Another thing to note is that they are also open ended. None of them are leading the designer or developer down a predetermined path of how to guide the user toward satisfying their goals.

This approach to defining the features of a product from the user needs leaves enough room for creativity when it comes to devising a solution, both for designers and developers. By creating a collection of user stories – referred to as a backlog in agile methodologies – written in this fashion, based on research of your users, the features of the product you are designing and building are provided with a set of guidelines that help you to shape the product to the needs and goals of the user, while leaving the details of how these features function and flow is left to those who specialize in design and development.

There are no restrictions placed on how a developer can utilize the technology at their disposal when building the solutions to a user story, just as there are none imposed on the designer when it comes to the user journey, the interaction design, or the user interface. Unfortunately, there is rarely a clean slate like this in larger organizations, and those constraints that are not introduced by the backlog of user stories arise from other areas of the organization, such as branding, design systems, pattern libraries, and existing architecture and frameworks that have been widely adopted.

Sometimes these constraints and the requirements of the business can find their way into user stories, which, quite frankly, is not where they belong.

Non-user Stories

> As a data analyst, I want to tag all interactions so that we can build a picture of how users use the app.

> As a developer, I want to refactor part of the code base so that it adheres to DRY principles.

> As a tester, I want all of the test cases defined so that I can ensure we cover everything in testing.

All of these examples of stories are similar to ones that I have come across while working in agile environments in a product or feature team. They are very much like user stories as they follow the same "as an <actor>" formatting. But there is one key difference. None of them are from the perspective of the user. None of them directly address the needs, tasks, or goals of those who will be using the product. If you already noticed this, great! You're already placing more importance and focus on user needs.

These "non-user" stories – or stakeholder stories – can be quite common in organizations that utilize agile methodologies for development. With the lack of a full functional specification that you would traditionally find in waterfall methodologies, the needs of the business find their way in among the user stories.

The reason I'm bringing attention to this muddling of stories in the backlog is that it can become very easy to lose the perspective of the user when the user stories become lost among the stakeholder stories. The prioritization of user needs above those of the business is easily forgotten if a developer or designer places equal weight against both types of story, or worse, prioritizes the needs of the stakeholders over those of the user.

As we have covered in earlier chapters, the needs of the user should be first and foremost in our minds if we are to create a better user experience, but there is always a balance to be struck in being able to deliver to the needs of the business and its stakeholders. As a developer, you should be looking to avoid requesting or writing user stories that reference the need to implement something in a certain way, or that you must build in some piece of functionality purely for internal purposes, or even just for your own benefit. While these may be important pieces of work, if they are not outrightly for the benefit of the user, they should not be contained within a user story. By all means, track them by some other method, but to conflate them deliberately with a user story is to devalue user stories as a whole.

Deriving Use Cases from User Stories

In my experience, use cases have often been conflated with user stories. Although they contain similar kinds of information (albeit a user story being far vaguer in comparison to a use case), they are created from different perspectives. The user story is generated from the needs of the user: who the user is, what they want, and why they want it.

A use case is written from the perspective of the system; its interactions with its users as well as interactions between internal components. From a developer's point of view, the use case is far more valuable in offering a set of guidelines on how to build out a specific flow or function in a digital product.

A use case consists of far more detail than the single statement found in a user story; at the very least a use case will comprise the following elements:

- **Name:** a short descriptor that outlines the scope of the use case.

- **Brief Description:** A paragraph to describe the full scope of the use case.

- **Actors:** Who or what (the user or other parts of the system) interacts with the system to achieve the goal.

- **Preconditions:** The state of the system prior to the events that occur in this use case.

- **Success Scenario:** The steps the actors follow in order to accomplish the goal of the use case.

- **Exceptions:** Captures less-common interactions between the actors and the system, including error and exceptions.

- **Post-conditions:** The state of the system following all of the events that occur in this use case.

Although use cases can be valuable tools to a developer and give a far more detailed insight into a particular journey or function, they are not focused upon the needs of the user, and as such, should be utilized in a way that complements the user story associated with the same journey or function. Use cases are a way to define the behavior of a system in order to meet the needs of the user as conveyed through user stories. As long as you bear in mind the user and the story to which a use case is related, you can avoid deviating from the goals of building your features and products for your users.

Utilizing Scenarios to Create a Narrative

Once we have personas that represent our various user groups and user stories to help us to understand what tasks they need to complete and why, what else do we need to build a more complete picture, a deeper understanding of our users, so that we can create a real connection with them, to empathize with them?

Scenarios can be described as the narrative in which a persona will be looking to achieve their goals as described in a user story. They describe the context of the user, why they come to use your website or application, and more importantly, the narrative that surrounds them. While it may sound rather excessive to create all-encompassing narratives around each of our user types (our personas), it is imperative to the enduring success of your personas and to sustaining a level of empathy for the user, both within the team and for yourself.

The Importance of Storytelling

Storytelling is the most fundamental way in which human beings have been communicating for thousands of years. It is an extraordinarily powerful way to engage other people, and our brains have evolved in such a way that it is hardwired to think in a way that connects cause and effect; we think in narratives.

Our brains become more engaged when being told a story than when, let's say, having a set of bullet points read out in a presentation. In the latter situation, our brain simply utilizes the parts that process language, but there is no reaction from the brain other than processing the words.

But when a story is told, colorful detail is used to describe the setting, the background of those people in the story, the how and reasons why they came to be there; the brain utilizes all of the areas that it would use as if the individual hearing the story were experiencing the events firsthand. The brain utilizes our own similar experiences that help us to relate to the story being told.

Those listening to the story become far more engaged and develop a real connection with the subject – in our case, this would be our user or persona – generating a deeper empathy for them and the context in which they find themselves.

Creating a Scenario

In order to create relevant and cohesive scenarios, we need to understand who the users are; their motivations and expectations; and their goals, which can all be derived from those elements we have walked through in this chapter

Creating scenarios adds further depth to the understanding we have built up of our users through our research and our efforts in generating empathy. They create the surrounding narrative in which our personas come to life.

Any scenario that is to be used to generate empathy with the user must answer three key questions:

- Who is the user?

- Why are they using your product?

- What are they trying to achieve?

Our personas will be able to provide the answer for who our user is, as well as provide some of the higher-level motivations. The user stories will give a more in-depth view of the user's motivations in more specific contexts and the goals they wish to accomplish. The personas and their associated user stories are the foundation for creating a scenario that ties everything together into a relatable narrative.

Instead of relying on a short user story that tells us the bare minimum of who the user is, what they want to do, and why they want to do it, an elaborated scenario will help the whole team to deliver a solution better suited to its users.

Let's take a look at one of the user stories we mentioned earlier in the chapter:

> As a current account holder, I want to quickly check my bank balance so that I can make sure I have enough money to buy the product I want.

Now let's take a look at what a fully formed scenario could be based on this user story, while considering a particular persona:

> Mr and Mrs Mooney are parents of three young children, two of which are in lower school, and the youngest has a place at nursery. Mrs Mooney is a nurse who works shift patterns; so organizing childcare is something that is always a priority. They have recently sold their house, and Mr Mooney left a full-time position to become an IT contractor with the money they made from their house sale. As an avid saver, Mrs X puts the vast majority of her salary directly into her savings account to prevent any unnecessary spending from her current account. However, when some kind of emergency spending is required – car repairs, for example – Mrs X will utilize her savings to pay for them. She is confident using modern technology, and will use her mobile phone to log in to her banking app to check if there is enough in her current account to pay for the repairs. If she does not have the required funds, she will transfer the necessary amount to her current account, from her savings, in order to pay the bill.

This kind of description of a real user – or indeed, a persona – creates a much greater feeling of understanding and empathy for the reader. Even by reading that scenario to yourself, you will have become more emotionally engaged with that user's story. Your brain will have used your own experiences to draw parallels with the user to help you better understand their situation, and to generate a better understanding, to generate empathy.

Scenarios are not necessarily something created by developers on a regular basis, and is not part of their job description, but once again we can argue that the more you understand your user, and the more you are able to empathize with them, the more able you are to build satisfying user experiences for them.

Keeping Empathy Alive

If you and your team are able to build empathy for your users using the methods we have gone through in this chapter, you will have created a great platform on which to build truly user-focused products.

With that said, the hardest part is to keep this empathy for the user alive: to always have the user in mind. While personas, user stories, and scenarios can create a deeper understanding of your users, the empathetic connection can easily be lost if they are not maintained. They need to become an intrinsic part of the process, part of the day to day.

To keep empathy alive, you will always have to be mindful of how your users will perceive, utilize, and behave with regard to the things you build. There should always be someone in the team who is there to represent the user. They should be the ones to question decisions on product design and development from the user's perspective, as they will not be there to make their own voice heard. If there is no one else in the team whose job it is to do this, the responsibility falls to you.

You can only successfully keep empathy for your users when your whole team becomes involved in a joint understanding of the user, their needs, and their motivations. You must constantly remind each other of how your personas behave in differing scenarios, and how the user stories your team create will push you toward the right approach, toward the best solution.

Now that you have an understanding, not only of the methods to generate empathy, but to hold that empathy for the user yourself, you are now one of the torchbearers. You are one of those who can now light the way for the others in your team when it comes to creating a real connection with your users: to creating empathy, maintaining it, and building better user experiences because of it.

Summary

There is no better way to gain empathy for your users than by sharing the same experience as them from their point of view. But as a developer, whether in a large organization or working as an individual, it can be difficult to gain exposure to your users in order to create this link of shared feelings and understanding. The methodologies we have covered in this chapter – from user research, through personas, user stories, and scenarios – will give you the insight you need to be able to understand your users in order to develop great user experiences, and some of the ways in which you can further the understanding of your user throughout your team.

CHAPTER 8

The Importance of Visual Design

If we cast our minds back to the very first chapter of this book, we took a look at the many disciplines that intersect to form part of what we know as User Experience Design. Although visual design is just one part of the larger whole, we should not underestimate its importance to the collective user experience. In this chapter we want to provide a better understanding of visual design, the psychology that underpins the visual design decisions that can be taken, and how accurately representing these design choices in the interfaces you build has a beneficial impact to the user experience.

Visual design is an instrument we use to communicate with the vast majority of people through a digital medium. The use of color, layout, spacing, illustrations, photography, icons, and typography forms the palette from which we can create the visual interfaces through which our users will engage with our products.

In a study carried out at Northumbria University, a number of online health sites were analyzed on how the content and design factors influenced the trust of the user. Of the feedback received from the participants, 94% was about the visual design, with only 6% regarding the content. The visual appeal and navigation methods had, by far, the biggest influence on the user's first impression of the site.

Another set of studies carried out by Dr. Gitte Lingaard at Carleton University looked to ascertain how quickly people form an opinion about the visual appeal of a web page based on colors, layout, perception of simplicity or complexity, how interesting or boring they found it, and whether they perceived it as good or bad design. The first two studies rated people's opinions after being presented with a website home page for 500 ms at a time. The third study did the same, but for only 50 ms. Throughout the three studies, the visual appeal ratings were highly correlated, meaning that visual appeal can be assessed by a user within 50 ms. This is a very small timeframe in which we must give

© Westley Knight 2019
W. Knight, *UX for Developers*, https://doi.org/10.1007/978-1-4842-4227-8_8

a good first impression to our users. The effects of this first impression cause a halo effect, or a cognitive confirmation bias where users then unwittingly search for evidence that confirms their initial reaction, while ignoring evidence to the contrary. Lingaard commented, "Even if a website is highly usable and provides very useful information presented in a logical arrangement, this may fail to impress a user whose first impression of the site was negative."

Both of these studies show us that a good implementation of visual design on a website can have a huge positive impact on the experience of the user. But isn't this the realm of the designer? Isn't it their job to create a compelling visual design so that our users become engaged with our product and develop trust with it by association?

Why Should Visual Design Matter to a Developer?

Just as the choices you make as to how you code a digital product can have an effect on the resulting user experience, the attention to detail when building a user interface from a visual design created by a designer can have the same impact. The ability to convert a functional specification into a working digital product does not alone make you a good developer. What makes a good developer is a more rounded set of skills, a larger understanding of the product you are building from more than your own perspective, and the ability to convert the intentions of the designers and the rest of the team into something that real people engage with. Figure 8-1 shows a comparison between the visual design provided by the designer and an implementation of that design in the browser. Although both images are very similar and contain the same elements, there are a number of discrepancies in the layout on the right that could induce negative reactions from the user when they see it for the first time, creating their perception of it being a "bad design."

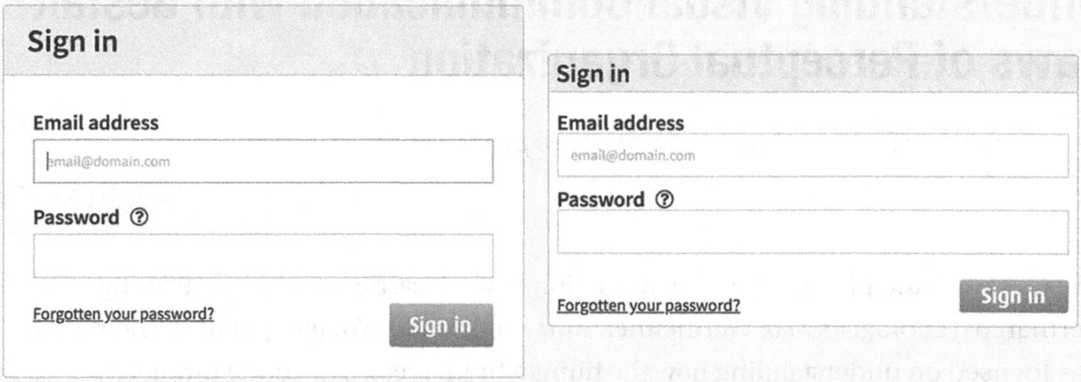

Figure 8-1. *An example of visual designer proved by the designer on the left in comparison with an implemented version of the design by a developer on the right*

If a user were to see the example on the right without prior knowledge of the original design on the left, as would happen in the real world, they would still be able to form a somewhat negative opinion of this layout. We will look more in depth at the principles behind visual communication and human perception, which will give us a greater understanding of why this kind of response occurs in our users, and how understanding these principles will help you to value the details in visual design that a designer does.

We should be sure to remember that the developer is the final piece in the puzzle when building digital products; the work they do brings the whole product to life. Just like a puzzle piece, if they aren't the right shape for their team, they don't fit in well enough to deliver that complete picture. By learning more about the other disciplines required to build a product, the developer can become a more valuable member of the team and be able to successfully deliver the intentions of the team as a whole.

Achieving this does not require a full understanding of every aspect of design. Just as a designer can learn some of the fundamentals of code and what is technically possible in terms of layout – without becoming a fully fledged front-end developer – you can utilize the fundamentals of design knowledge to close the divide between developers and designers. First, we should look to understand some of the psychology that underpins how we perceive visual stimuli, and how we can utilize this to deliver better visual interfaces for our users.

Understanding Visual Communication with Gestalt Laws of Perceptual Organization

The whole is other than the sum of the parts.

—Kurt Koffka

The Gestalt Principles are the consummation of work carried out in the 1920s by German psychologists Max Wertheimer, Kurt Koffka, and Wolfgang Kohler. Their work was focused on understanding how the human brain creates meaning through the perception of the chaotic stimuli that surrounds us: how the brain creates order from the huge variety of visual stimulus it receives.

The Law of Similarity

Elements that share superficial characteristics tend to be organized into groups, especially when seen within the context of a screen. Figure 8-2 below serves as an example of how a group forming bias unconsciously organizes the elements on display into a more meaningful associative context.

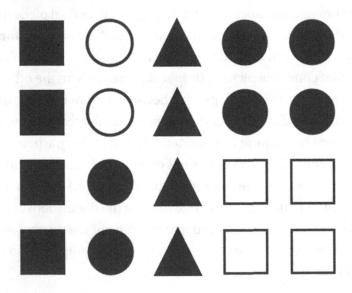

Figure 8-2. *A collection of simple geometric shapes that are grouped by our perception*

We are able to draw on the Law of Similarity in our visual designs by utilizing the similarity of shape, size, color, and orientation in the elements of an interface to provide them with a perceived relationship. On top of this, we are able to juxtapose certain elements within a perceived group of similar objects by creating an "anomaly": something that creates a focal point for a user to perceive as more important than the other similar objects with which it is grouped. With this we can point a user to a piece of important information or direct them to the action we want them to take next.

The Law of Proximity

The effect that the visual proximity of a number of objects has in terms of our perception of grouping them together is characterized under the Law of Proximity. If we take a look at Figure 8-3, we can see an example that features a number of dots arranged in different ways.

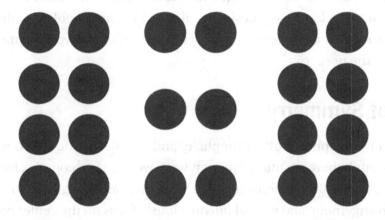

Figure 8-3. *A depiction of geometric objects grouped by our perception of proximity*

The Law of Proximity has an effect on our perception when we group two or more separate elements closely together. It is slower for us to detect distinct groups, or to determine which items belong to which group, when the proximity between objects is reduced to such an extent that there is no discernible difference between the intended groups to which the items belong. This can be found in websites and applications that do not adhere to the Law of Proximity, and corrected by utilizing whitespace effectively between elements that should and should not be associated.

The Law of Familiarity

Have you ever looked up to the sky and seen a cloud that looked like an animal, a face, or some another recognizable object? The law of familiarity is derived from the unconscious process that our brain uses to form mental representations the should-have use or relevance to us. Within the interfaces we create, we will build a number of components that are not only familiar to us but also you, our users. Components such as navigation, sidebars, carousels, content grids, and many more all have an air of familiarity about them for our users.

By following a common pattern for a specific type of interaction, an image gallery for example, the user will likely be familiar with how they should interact with this component and will therefore feel comfortable using it. If, however, we were to completely reinvent the functional and interactive elements of an image gallery, we would create an incongruous experience for the user; there would be inconsistency between their expectations from a more meaningful interface than an unfamiliar innovation.

The impact for developers and designers alike is that they should be mindful of utilizing innovative new approaches to preexisting patterns, in favor of something that is more familiar to the user.

The Law of Symmetry

The biases of our perception look for simplicity and symmetry when we view most objects, even though there are many different ways we can view complex forms. Our brains tend to group visual elements together when they are recognized to be in a symmetrical arrangement, and we will unconsciously focus on the center point so that the brain can extract the simplest form.

In terms of visual design, symmetry is visually pleasing and allows us to focus on what is important. With the law of symmetry, we are able to utilize a comparable approach to that we outlined with the Law of Similarity; we are able to add juxtaposing, asymmetrical elements to a page in order to bring the user's focus to those areas. Figure 8-4 depicts a high-level wireframe of different objects, with the thinner lines showing the line of symmetry between the objects.

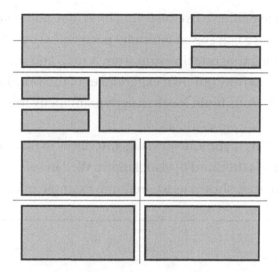

Figure 8-4. *A wireframe layout showcasing examples of symmetry*

The Law of Continuity

The ability for humans to perceive elements as a constant form in a particular direction, despite other possible bisecting, interlinking, or obstructing objects, is what forms the law of continuity. A common example used to illustrate this is shown in Figure 8-5 below.

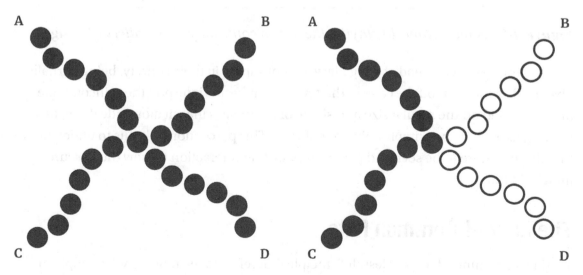

Figure 8-5. *An example of our perception of continuity*

On the left, we tend to perceive two bisecting lines, one going from A to D, the other from B to C. On the right, we can see an alternate perspective by differentiating the lines with visual styling, showing that one line runs from A to C, and the other from B to D.

This example illustrates how our own experiences of the world around us are heavily biased by the way in which our brain looks to derive simplicity from the complex visual input we receive.

We are able to apply this technique to visual interfaces to take advantage of the way in which our brains process this kind of visual input. We can see this technique often applied to a gallery of images, shown as a wireframe example in Figure 8-6 below.

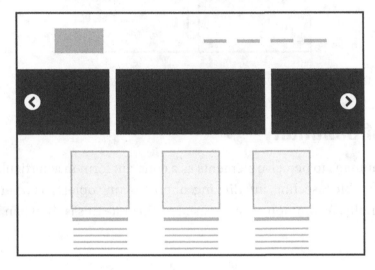

Figure 8-6. *A wireframe displaying the law of continuity for a gallery of images*

The images at each end of the gallery are not shown in their entirety, being partially obscured as they run off the edge of the screen. Our brains interpret these incomplete images, based on the regular size and shape of the images that sit alongside them, as existing as a whole but simply being out of view. This perception helps us to understand that there is more to be seen and can prompt further interaction to view the obscured images in full.

The Law of Common Fate

The law of common fate is a Gestalt Principle that refers to the tendency for people to group elements together that are perceived as moving in the same direction. An example of this in nature would be a flock of migrating birds; although the flock is made up of a large number of individual birds, they are perceived as a whole as they are traveling at the same speed and in the same direction.

Applying the law of common fate in our interfaces gives the user the perception that the objects moving together, or as a result of their interaction with certain elements resulting in that movement, are related.

The accentuated areas in Figure 8-7 below depict a number of elements that may utilize the law of common fate to good effect. The use of animation within a navigation menu for child pages that appear in a drop-down menu consolidates the perception that all of the drop-down below each item are all related. We can also see a similar effect within an accordion style list; each option expanding with the interaction of the user to show more detail.

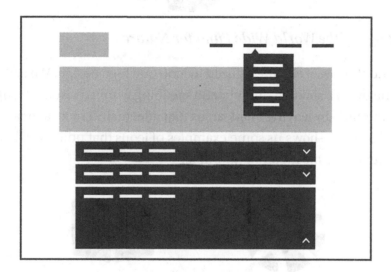

Figure 8-7. *A wireframe highlighting a drop-down menu and an accordion component*

The Law of Closure

With the brain looking to make sense of the visual input in the most efficient way possible, the law of closure describes the perceptual bias through which we are able to create meaningful, whole objects, despite limited visual information. Figure 8-8 below shows the World Wide Fund for Nature logo, which utilizes basic geometric shapes with blank areas. Our brain is able to process the apparently missing information to perceive a meaningful whole, which in this case is a panda bear.

Figure 8-8. *Logo of the World Wide Fund for Nature*

We often find the law of closure utilized in icon and logo design. We can take advantage of the brain's ability to understand meaning within a visual by implying the existence of something by leaving blank areas that effectually create a meaningful whole to the viewer. Figure 8-9 shows us some examples of icons that utilize the law of closure to help the viewer to see the meaningful whole.

Figure 8-9. *Examples of icons that utilize closure from FontAwesome*

By reducing complexity in our visual layouts and taking advantage of the human brain's natural abilities outlined in the Gestalt Principles, we can reduce cognitive load, making it easier for the user to concentrate on the things we want them to, rather than trying to untangle complex interfaces and having to make a real effort to try to understand how to use what they see in front of them.

Working with Trends in Visual Design

In the same manner that we should not pick up the latest JavaScript framework and just start building the next feature or product with this new technology, we must be mindful of new trends that can emerge on a constant basis in our industry.

As with any framework or new method of working, we must evaluate it on a number of aspects. Will it be supported far into the future? How much technical debt will the shift to a new approach create? Do the benefits outweigh the costs? Is there a big learning curve for your team? All of these questions, and so many more, should be considered when looking to adopt a new technology or approach to working.

The same is true for visual design. Many of these same questions that we aim at the developers, the product team, and the business – to determine whether or not a new technology should be utilized – can be reframed to ask similar questions on behalf of our users in terms of the trends we may be tempted to follow and the visual language we use to communicate with them.

Over the years we have seen large shifts in the directions taken with the aesthetics of digital interfaces. One of the more well-known examples of this kind of shift was in 2013 when Apple unveiled their new look operating system for the iPhone. The move from iOS6 to iOS7 sparked huge debate in the design community by moving from a skeuomorphic visual design to a "flat" aesthetic as show in Figure 8-10 below.

Figure 8-10. *A comparison of home screens between iOS6 and iOS7*

In 2014, Google reinforced this change in digital visual design with the release of Material Design, their card-based design system with responsive animations, transitions, and the addition of depth to an otherwise flat aesthetic, without attempting to relate the visuals back to the real world like the skeuomorphic approach.

Although two of the most dominant companies in the mobile digital arena moved toward this preferred application of visual design, it was not without its issues when applied to the wider audience of the World Wide Web. As the trend took hold, many brands looked to embrace this new aesthetic, copying from the industry leaders, without necessarily following best practices in order to help their users. Prior to this visual shift, people have become accustomed to the way in which interactive elements were presented to them; links would predominantly be blue and underlined, and buttons would look more like real-world buttons. By immediately removing these familiar elements in pursuit of a new visual direction, this has huge implications for your users, and as a result will reflect on the business.

The Gestalt Principles we have walked through still stand when it comes to the interfaces you build with the latest and greatest ways of approaching your implementation. Regardless of how important a designer may see this shift to keep up with modern trends, it pales into insignificance when compared to the real needs of the user.

Design Principles for Usability

In order to successfully navigate the constant ebb and flow of visual design trends across the web and native platforms, we can utilize Don Norman's design principles for usability. In his book *The Design of Everyday Things* (Basic Books, 1988), Don introduced some basic interface design principles that can help us to negotiate the ever-changing visual landscape of digital interfaces across varying platforms.

Consistency

Consistency for the user – not just within your product, but in keeping with the rest of the World Wide Web and native platforms – is key to effectively communicating with the user. By utilizing similar elements that have similar operations to those found elsewhere across digital products, your user can recognize and recall how to interact with these patterns, reducing their cognitive load and making it easier for the user to complete their tasks within your product.

Consistency within your own application or website, whether that is through the visual brand, interface patterns, or preferably a combination of both, is key to building trust with your users. Inconsistency causes confusion, especially when two different elements are presented in the same visual manner do not behave in the same way from a user's interaction. This results in the user having to apply more effort to learn the exceptions to the rules, creating a greater cognitive load, which causes a negative emotional response from the user.

Being consistent in a way that avoids the user having to work harder to understand how to use your interface fosters a sense of trustworthiness and avoids alienating your users.

Visibility

Simply put, this is making sure that all of the ways that a user can interact with an interface can be discovered visually by the user. The controls that are available to the user should be clear and obvious, again reducing the amount of work the user has to do to understand how to interact with what is presented to them. By hiding controls, or placing them in expected areas, this decreases usability and makes it harder for the user to learn how to interact with the interface.

At the other end of the scale, we should be mindful as to not include *all* of the possible interactions with a product on a single screen. Doing so can simply cause cognitive overload and result in the user experience choice paralysis: the inability for the user to select the option they require in a vast array of choices.

Affordance

Affordance is the name given to the visual characteristics of an element that provide the user with clues as to how to interact with that element. A common example of this in a digital interface would be that of a button.

For example, if the function of the button is to submit a form, the aesthetics of the button must provide a visual clue to the user that they are able to click or tap it in order to submit their form. This can be done visually by making the digital button look like a real-world button by using a three-dimensional look, or by creating an obvious visual difference to all other elements in the same interface so that the user understands that the button will act as the user expects.

Another example of this is the humble hyperlink. In any text viewed on any website, if we were to see a few words highlighted in blue with an underline of the same color, the user immediately recognizes this pattern and understands what will happen when they interact with it.

Feedback

By providing the user with feedback following an interaction with an element on the screen, this provides the user with confirmation that their intended action has been carried out, whether done successfully or unsuccessfully. But if we were to leave the user in a state of limbo, by not providing a confirmation of their action, even if the intended action did indeed happen, the user is left without any knowledge as to the success or failure of their action. Without feedback, we can easily foster a sense of mistrust, simply because we are not informing the user when something happens in relation to their interactions.

Mapping

Using visual cues as to what will happen when a user interacts with a given element in a digital interface helps the user to understand what effect that interaction will have. By creating a relationship between an interactive element and the effect it will have, we create a mapping that the user can interpret from an explicit visual prompt. In digital interfaces, this can be done by utilizing known conventions form the real world, such as a button being given a three-dimensional look as we mentioned when talking about affordance. Alternatively, these can be general conventions in digital interfaces, such as accordions that expand and contract to show more or less information as the user selects an option from a list, or perhaps that clicking the logo on a website will take you to the home page.

Constraints

Finally, constraints can be used to help the user avoid making mistakes within an interface. We can help prevent invalid data being entered into a form, and prevent invalid actions being performed. An example of this would be to disable or remove inputs in a form that are not required for the user to continue their task, or to prevent a user landing halfway through a multistep process without providing the required data in previous steps.

These five principles help us to form a basic understanding of what makes a digital product more usable and provide a platform on which we can build modern solutions to make the lives of our users easier, as well as those of our developers.

How Design Patterns Benefit Developers

Design patterns help us to be more efficient in delivering screen designs and functionality. With a set of shared, predefined patterns to build our interfaces, we rarely have to build anything from scratch, improving the efficiency in building out larger interfaces comprising of several components from a pattern library or larger design system. When we are required to create a pattern or component that does not yet exist in our library, we are able to spend our time more effectively in creating a component that will integrate and work alongside all of the preexisting components in our library.

A shared pattern library, complete with code snippets, enables the developers and designers across an organization, to utilize each other's components and patterns, reducing the amount of duplicate work, especially when the same component can be coded in a large variety of ways, using any number of different approaches to structure and syntax.

By utilizing the design system as a repository of coding standards for existing components, we can improve the quality of code that all developers deliver throughout an organization, regardless of internal team structures or physical location. There is an inherent consistency that arises from utilizing a shared pattern library that enhances the readability of code, simplifies the development process, and creates a more robust code base through the ongoing improvement to components as they evolve over time to meet the demands required of them.

As design patterns obviously help both designers and developers in quite a variety of ways, what benefits do they give to the user?

How Design Patterns Benefit Our Users

The patterns that we create within a design system for our product aim to follow the five principles of designing for usability that we walked through earlier in the chapter: consistency, visibility, affordance, feedback, and constraints. When combined with the human psychology-based Gestalt Principles, we take advantage of the way human beings are predisposed to process visual stimuli, and we reduce the cognitive load required for a user to navigate our products, complete their tasks, and reach their goals.

By utilizing common interface visual design and functionality, we reduce the need for our user to spend energy thinking about how they should interact with a given component, and what their expectations are in terms of the functions they provide. Let's take a look at some examples of common patterns we may find across the web.

Pagination is a common component utilized across many different types of websites and can be commonly found in search engines, forums, and retail websites. The examples in Figure 8-11 below show how the same pattern can be visually different, but that there are enough similarities for us to recognize this pattern and how we except it to function.

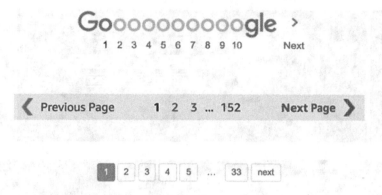

Figure 8-11. *A collection of pagination patterns from Google, Amazon, and Stack Overflow*

All of the derivatives of the same pattern share common elements. They all display numbers to represent the pages through which the user can navigate and include a next button to navigate to the next set of content. Amazon and Stack Overflow also include an ellipsis within the list of pages to represent the multiple pages in between the first few on display, and then jump to the final page number to provide the user with the total number of pages available to them. All of them highlight the current page that the user is on and remove the link from that option so that the user cannot click the link to the page they are already on, which could lead to confusion for the user by landing on the same page they were just on.

Another example of a pattern utilized across the web and in applications is the carousel. Figure 8-12 below shows us the carousels that can be found in iTunes, on the Netflix website, and on Amazon's home page.

Figure 8-12. *A collection of carousel patterns from iTunes, Netflix, and Amazon*

All of these examples show a clear set of navigation arrows to the left and right of the content on display, providing the user with a means to manually traverse the content. The carousels on iTunes and Amazon are animated and will move from right to left to show the user that there is more content beyond that which they are currently viewing. Both iTunes and Netflix show partial pieces of content that overrun the edges of the screen, utilizing the Gestalt Law on continuation to inform the user that there is more content, without having to automate the scroll from one are to the next, although iTunes employs both of these mechanics.

Although these examples are different both visually and in some aspects of functionality, the common underlying pattern means that the user is immediately familiar with how to interact with these components, and what they expect to happen as a result.

Using Animation

Another aspect of visual design comes in the form of motion. Often overlooked as a significant part of visual design on the web, and as a possible positive influence on the user experience, animation in user interfaces can provide direction to the user, reduce their cognitive load, communicate changes in status, and deliver useful contextual feedback. In order for animation within a user interface to be able to achieve this, they must be functional and meaningful, not frivolous and impractical. They must provide useful information; they must feel like a response to the actions of the user; and if they do both of these well, they can trigger an emotional response, creating a deeper engagement from the user.

In order for animation to contribute successfully to the improvement of a user experience, it must be considered early in the software development life cycle; it cannot be an afterthought. Developers can provide a guiding hand to the designers on the art of the possible when it comes to implementing animations in the user interfaces when they become involved with the design process. The developer's level of knowledge of the possibilities of animation when utilizing CSS and JavaScript, or the frameworks their applications are built upon, can determine the level and variety of animations that are possible to achieve. Designers should be considering the animations of their components, transitions between screens, and visual feedback from interactions before a pixel is placed on a digital canvas, so they must engage with the developers to understand what their technological constraints are.

Just as a designer should consider animation to be an integral part of the user experience, developers should also see it as an integral part of writing code. It is no longer a nice-to-have addition to your core product, neither is it only an aesthetic element. The traditional focus of the developer to deliver functionality that enables the user to complete their task is no longer enough on its own as static interfaces are now largely a thing of the past. A digital product released today that lacks this functional animation will immediately look and feel dated.

When animation is considered by designers – with the guidance of developers – in the early design phases as an integral part of the product, we find that the animations themselves are used to convey meaning; they serve a purpose. Any interface that has been completed in terms of visual design without any consideration for the purpose of animations can end up applying them as the metaphorical icing on the cake, merely as a decorative effect. These kinds of animations are ultimately unnecessary and can impede the user rather than enhance their experience.

The reason animations should be considered before any digital interface designs are created is because they should serve a purpose. Unlike the "icing on the cake" animations mentioned above, functional animations benefit the user and help our users to process the visual information more efficiently. Let's take a look at the five roles that animation serves in our user interfaces.

Affordance

As we have discussed earlier in this chapter, affordance in digital interfaces helps the user to understand what they can interact with on a screen, how to interact with it, and, in some part, the expected outcome of that interaction. Animation can be utilized to further accentuate the affordance of a digital element in view of the user. Referring back to our carousel examples in Figure 8-12, we mentioned how both iTunes and Amazon use animation to move between items of content within a confined space. This animation highlights to the user that there is more content beyond what they initially see and enhances the affordance of the navigation buttons.

This is exemplified by the Netflix interface. In Figure 8-13 below, we can see the beginning state of the interface for the web-based version of the Netflix app. As the user hovers over a title, it expands into a large area of content shown in the central image, layering text and interactive icons over the top. This interaction, which occurs without the user making the decision to click on it, informs the user that this element can be interacted with further, and in different ways with the visual cues provided by the icons show in context with that title.

Figure 8-13. *An example of the different states of the Netflix web-based interface, with the initial state shown on the left and the hover state on the right*

Focus

Although we can utilize animations to draw the focus of the user to a specific element on the screen, we must be careful of our implementation. Animation used at the wrong time or in the wrong place can distract the user from their task at hand. If they are reading through an article, a sudden animation of a new element in to view can distract the user, creating a negative emotional response.

When used correctly, in the use of a notification following specific user-initiated actions, for example, it can be a vehicle for providing reassurance to the user, as we only require their attention to be drawn to a message at that time, for a small duration, and for a specific and relevant reason. Another example, albeit a little more of a gimmick, is the animation that moves an icon from the "Add to cart" button up to the shopping cart when a user adds an item to their cart. It provides visual reinforcement that the item they have selected has been added to their cart.

Feedback

Just as in the example above where we mentioned notifications that can draws the user's attention to them in the right situation, this is also an example of how we can provide feedback to the user. For example, a user may have amended a setting in their preferences, under their account settings in your product. We can provide a confirmation notification that the action has been carried out behind the scenes or return an error if there has been a problem. We can also provide more immediate feedback with approaches like inline validation on forms, highlighting form fields where the users' input does not match the required criteria of required data such as email addresses or passwords.

Figure 8-14 shows the feedback provided by the Dropbox website when uploading a file. The feedback in the form of a progress bar is displayed during the upload in the image on the left, while the image on the right shows the change of the notification to a confirmation once the upload has been completed.

Figure 8-14. *Feedback notifications shown on the Dropbox website while uploading a file*

Orientation

Animation between states and pages is becoming more and more common and is now almost expected, especially with touch interfaces on mobile devices. Animations that aid orientation for the user are often a visual representation of the hierarchy of the information architecture of a product. It is common to see horizontal sliding transitions when switching between options in a mobile navigation bar that sits at the bottom of the screen, and as you move from one option to the next, the content area also transitions to mimic the same movement the user has made between sections. For example, In Apple's iOS 12 for their range of mobile devices, specifically on iPhone X shown in Figure 8-15, the user can swipe up from the bottom of the screen to reveal the other apps they have open at the time, and easily swipe and tap to switch to a different app.

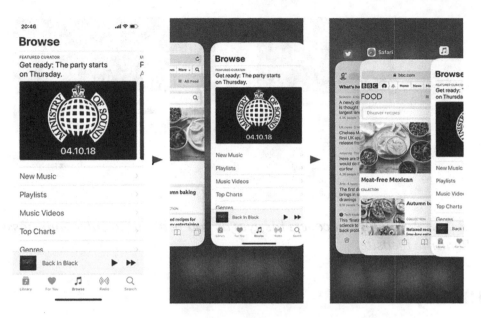

Figure 8-15. *The stages of animation in iOS as a user swipes up from the bottom of their device in order to swipe through their open apps*

Delight

Although animation is becoming a vital part of digital user interfaces and must first and foremost be functional and help to guide the user on their way, there is no reason that these animations should not surprise and delight the user. Although this may seem like the frivolity that renders animation more annoying than useful, used well it can serve as a way to reinforce your brand, keep your user engaged, and even generate positive emotions, lending to a better overall experience with your product. The Readme website provides a delightful touch to their login screen, illustrated in Figure 8-16. On the login page, there is an owl peeking over your login form. As your cursor lays focused on the password field, the owl covers their eyes so not to see what you're typing. Although it is nothing more than a fun piece of animation, when a user recalls the Readme website simply down to this fun little interaction, it becomes very valuable indeed.

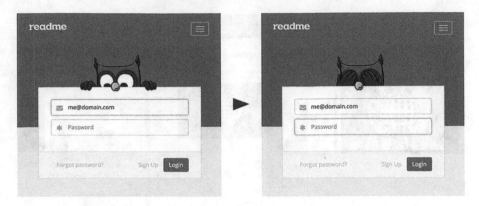

Figure 8-16. *A playful owl covers his eyes as you're about to enter your password on the Readme website*

Summary

In this chapter we have looked at why visual design is so important to the user experience. We have covered a number of psychological principles that help us to understand why our own brains perceive visual input in the way they do, and how we translate that into useful information that can be understood and acted upon. We looked at why visual design should be of importance to a developer, and how the use of style guides, pattern libraries, and all-encompassing design systems can help not only developers and designers, but the wider organization, as well as the benefits they provide to creating a more robust and reliable user experience. Finally, we took a look at how animation plays a part alongside the visual design, and how it can be an integral part of the visual design and how we communicate with our users.

CHAPTER 9

Prototype, Evaluate, Iterate

As we have talked about a lot of the theory and psychology behind user experience design, and why it's important for developers to realize how much of an effect this can have on our users – which in turn reflects on our products – we must move on to how we can implement these learnings in our daily work, and specifically how we can use our development skills to benefit our products by lending them to different aspects of the software development life cycle.

As the title of this chapter alludes to, we will be looking specifically at how developers can be involved in prototyping during the early phases of design and development, how we evaluate those prototypes in order to gain insight from our users, and how we can utilize an iterative design process to continually improve our products and the way in which we build them.

First, we will look at the iterative design process as a whole before we go into the details of prototyping and evaluation that are encapsulated within that model.

The Iterative Design Process

The general concept of the iterative design process is not a particularly complex one. Once the needs of the user and the business have been established, the product team will enter an initial planning phase, as depicted in Figure 9-1 below. The team then moves into a cyclical process of defining requirements for this cycle or sprint, followed by analysis, design, and implementation. Once the requirements have been met, the product is deployed either to a live environment or perhaps one for test purposes, and the team can then carry out usability testing and evaluation of the product, which informs the next cycle of the design process.

© Westley Knight 2019
W. Knight, *UX for Developers*, https://doi.org/10.1007/978-1-4842-4227-8_9

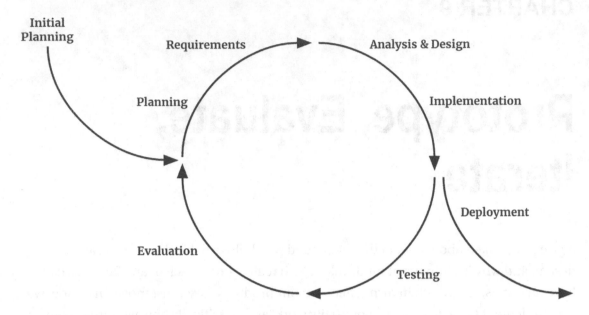

Figure 9-1. *A depiction of the iterative design process*

The reason I mention both live and test environments depends on how your team and the business wish to deliver its products to its users. We could first deliver many iterations into a test environment that could be put through usability testing with a handful of users in order to inform the product team of issues and needs that were not original discovered, before we release a product into the world that does not satisfy the needs of the user.

The benefits of the iterative process, in conjunction with releases to a non-live environment, is that we are able to reduce the number of usability problems by conducting usability testing sessions, avoiding the negative impacts that can occur by releasing our products untested, with unknown usability problems. It is near impossible to design and build without any usability problems on the first attempt, even with the most experienced designers and developers working on a product.

The iterative process is not just doing the same work over and over again, with a vague hope that something improves following that repeated process. It is actually centered around continuous delivery: the ability to build out an MVP, release that to your users, use that to gather data on how your users interact with it in the real world, and then utilize that data to improve your product. Iterating on design in this way, building prototypes, and performing usability testing, both before and after release, are the methods that help us to understand the usability issues our users will experience, allows us to correct them efficiently, and helps reduce the amount of risk and negative impact we may have experienced without this process.

According to Jakob Nielsen, iterating through at least three versions of an interface is recommended, and user testing can substantially improve usability. In four case studies, the overall improvement in usability was measured at 165% from first iteration to last, and the median improvement per iteration was 38%. These measurements can be derived from different metrics during usability testing, such as the reduction in time taken to complete a task, the reduction in number of errors made by the user, or the subjective satisfaction of the user.

The Minimum Viable Product

In today's world of design and development, there is an emphasis placed on delivering the Minimum Viable Product (MVP) in order to satisfy the core needs of the user to garner feedback in order to improve the product through future releases, and this approach fits very well within the iterative design methodology. Unfortunately, this approach does have its pitfalls – just as any methodology will have when implemented in teams – and there are elements that can be taken advantage of that do not help us to deliver to the needs of the user.

With MVPs, we must remember that the keyword is "viable." This is not meant to be viable for the organization to spend time and money with an expected return on that investment. No, the focus is that the product should be viable to the user; it must cater to their needs and help them to complete their goals.

Many development teams that keep their focus firmly on efficiency and the ability to deliver can easily lose sight of what is viable to release to the user, and can instead concentrate firmly on the "minimum." This may or may not be a problem within your team or your business, but it tends to flourish in those organizations that find themselves in the lower levels of UX maturity. In an attempt to try to change the focus of the developer and the wider team from only developing something viable with the minimum amount of work, some have come to replace the word "viable" with the word "valuable" within the MVP acronym. The intention of this is to shift the focus from the developers on to the users. Rather than releasing a product or feature that just about "makes the grade" for the users of a MVP, the minimum valuable product must deliver value to its user; it must satisfy their needs in order to be something that is viable for them to use.

When Minimum Viable Products Don't Deliver

One example of the "viable" taking precedent over the "valuable" was the initial release of the Adobe XD application. Pitched as a streamlined solution to deal with user interface design, interaction design, and prototyping all rolled into one, I had high hopes for this product, as did many members of the UX community. The hope was for a product that would replace the multiple applications in a UX designer's daily workflow, meaning that they wouldn't have to move between Axure, Sketch, Principle, Framer, or any number of other productivity tools. Unfortunately, the early releases of Adobe XD fell short of delivering to those requirements, both in my own eyes and to many in the UX community, with my own first attempt at using in Adobe XD was to build a prototype of a relatively straightforward form. I soon discovered that I could not create any interactive form elements – at least not without a huge amount of work to replicate that kind of functionality – meaning that the basic functional aspects of the prototype I was looking to build was just not achievable; the product was not a viable solution to me as a user.

The message here is not to show Adobe XD in a bad light – that piece of software has come on leaps and bounds since its initial release. However, it does highlight the difference between what a product team may consider viable – in that it can carry out the very basic of task for a user to do the bare minimum – but it does not then offer the value to the user. That value will be the driving factor behind the adoption of your product, its continued use, creating evangelists for your product, all of which will come together to bring long-lasting success.

UX Benefits from the MVP

Whichever way you may look at delivering an MVP, the aim is the same: to improve your product with continuous cycles of design and development, followed by testing and evaluation in order to feed the next cycle in the advancement of your product.

The benefits of this process are not only for the user who gets regular updates to a product that improves over time – helping them to complete their tasks and achieve their goals – it has benefits for the business and the whole team that work on the product. The fact that we are looking to deliver MVPs more often means that we are inherently building in the capacity to make changes to functionality and requirements as we progress. It's this constant and immediate improvement that must come after each delivery, after each release. Basing the changes to the product on the feedback from usability testing and analytics allow us to make those changes much earlier in the shorter cycles of the iterative design process, especially when compared to delivering a much larger piece of work in a larger timeframe. The makes any mistakes less costly while they are in the wild, and reduces the cost of fixing these issues on this relatively small scale.

Prototyping

Prototyping is a way in which organizations are able to get an idea of how a feature or product may look and function like without spending a great deal of time and money to create the finished article. The iterative design process places a focus on the ability to rapidly prototype solutions catering to user needs. This facilitates the ability to continuously test your prototype with real users, discovering usability issues and flaws in design that could otherwise go undiscovered, and even make it into your products release.

The rapid nature of the iterative design process in conjunction with prototyping can find designers utilizing low-fidelity prototypes in the discovery phase to help shape the direction of a product. Low-fidelity prototyping traditionally involves non-interactive prototypes, often paper based, allowing the designers to create varying possible solutions to a user's need, while not investing large amounts of time and effort in order to improve upon a product.

High-fidelity prototyping is where the developer can have a significant degree of impact. This is where prototyping for digital applications and websites becomes computer-based and interactive. These prototypes aim to represent the user interface as closely as possible to a true representation of what the product will look and feel like as it would be when complete. The closer a high-fidelity prototype appears in comparison to a production-ready user interface, the more effective we can be at collecting true-to-life data from our users during usability testing. There is an additional benefit in that we can also use these high-fidelity prototypes to demonstrate the product to our own stakeholders.

The higher the fidelity, the more connected to the product a user can feel. The higher the degree of realistic interaction between the user and the digital product, we are able to more accurately assess the needs of those users when they are engaged with an interface that produces feedback based on their interactions, generating mental, physical, and emotional responses from the user. This provides us with insights into what we could do to make our products more usable, and perhaps more importantly, the reasons why. As a developer you have the knowledge and tools to build these high-fidelity prototypes, meaning that you are more closely connected to the user than maybe you possibly thought. This is the opportunity that you can grasp in order to better understand your users, and to discover how your work really has an impact on their experience with your product.

The Four Prototyping Process Models

Aside from the high and low fidelities, there are four main approaches to prototyping for software development, all of which can be carried out by developers, but some will be more valuable than others depending on the scenario you may find yourselves. In relation to the type of product you are building, the methodologies that your development team follows, and even with your own personal preference of how you would like to work, you will be able to follow one of these methodologies to help facilitate prototyping for your team. You will gain the benefits of creating usable pieces of software to validate ideas before building production-ready products at higher costs of time and effort.

Throw-Away Prototyping

Also known as rapid prototyping, throw-away prototyping involves the creation of a rough prototype built with a bare minimum set of requirements and user goals. The idea is to utilize this prototype to generate a more thorough understanding of user needs, and a more refined set of requirements as a result. This type of prototyping is commonly viewed as a waste of a developer's time: having them code something up that will only be valuable for a short period of time and discarded shortly afterward. As a result, this type of prototyping is mainly carried out by designers, utilizing software to build out partially functioning examples of a particular journey or feature. With the focus of this kind of prototyping being the validation of needs and goals, and a tool to further define the requirements of a feature or product, this method of prototyping can require little to no developer input without any negative impact when used in the ideation phase of a project.

Evolutionary Prototyping

The evolutionary model of prototyping lends itself well to the MVP approach adopted by the majority of product teams. It utilizes a well-defined and thoroughly understood set of requirements in order to build a nascent prototype, satisfying the prioritized requirements to deliver an initial MVP that is of value to the user. Once the product is released, through feedback and testing we are able to improve upon the initial prototype, building upon that foundation to slowly evolve the product over time to deliver to the goals of the users and the business.

This method of prototyping requires a huge amount of collaboration between the designers and developers, and it is really where a developer's understanding of user experience can truly help the resulting product to flourish. In conjunction with the larger iterative design process, evolutionary prototyping places the designers and developers in a position to work very closely, with each benefiting from the other's experience. If you haven't yet had the chance to work like this as a developer, it is one of the fastest ways in which you will develop an understanding of user experience design, and in return you will foster an understanding of the development process with your team.

With the progressive nature of this approach, there is a constant need to refine the product, which means that the developer is not beholden to a grand scheme with specific goal posts that are set in stone at the outset of a project. It allows the team to concentrate on building what matters to the user, and means that they are not being held to account when there is any kind of deviation from the original plan. The prototypes created by working in this manner can often become the foundation for the code that ends up in the release version of the product. Even though it may be the case that the prototype evolves into part of the final product, it must always be regarded as a prototype as it will likely only hold functionality for the area of the product that is being worked on, and not a full solution to all of the possible user needs that you will be looking to address.

Incremental Prototyping

An incremental prototyping approach shares many of the characteristics with one main difference; there is not one prototype, but many in development at the same. Each of these prototypes may be addressing different features, user journeys, or individual pages of an app or website. The ultimate goal is to bring all of these prototypes together into the overall digital product.

Again, this approach fits nicely with iterative design, and each prototype is run in its own iterative design process, independently of the others. This can be a complicated process and requires a large amount of communication, not just between the different disciplines within each team, but between all of the teams to make sure that they are working to create a cohesive product as a whole. With multiple streams of work in progress at the same time, the risks of creating a fractured user experience – as each team's approach to solving a similar type of problem may be wildly different – become far greater without good management of the multiple teams, shepherding of the problem-solving approaches, and the use of accepted design patterns from an agreed-upon pattern library or design system. However, should these potential pitfalls be successfully negotiated, the one huge advantage that can be gained is the significant reduction in time from the start of the project to the delivery of the final product.

Extreme Prototyping

Consisting of three stages of work, extreme prototyping starts out with a static prototype built with HTML, CSS, and perhaps a little JavaScript thrown in to build out the user interface. These screens are then enhanced by integrating them with a simulated services layer, essentially a set of test data upon which the prototype can be evolved into a working version of the product, albeit without live APIs or other back-end services. In the third phase, these services are then added to bring the product into its release state.

Although the "extreme" aspect of this method of prototyping accelerates the project life cycle and reduces time to delivery, it has been known to cause problems where the developers are creating functional UIs without guidance. Again, this problem can be resolved by developers working closely with designers. The expertise that the front-end developer can lend to the first phase of this process can help to guide the user experience from the outset. Rather than the UI that is created in this first stage driving the functionality of the product, by working closely with UX designers, the developer/ designer pairing can result in the extremely efficient development of a conceptual experience from the mind's eye of the designer, into a usable – albeit static – version of the resulting user experience of the product.

This approach also helps to keep the team focused on delivering the functionality that tends to the needs of the user, rather than uncovering a wide variety of requirements that could end up bloating the product with unnecessary features. Again, this approach works well when looking to deliver an MVP to the user, with the focus on the value that the product would provide for its users. It is usually a rather hectic time when a team chooses to take this approach, but the value for both the business and the user can be realized much more quickly, and the stages of this particular prototyping process lends itself to performing regular usability testing to validate ideas, interaction designs, and functionality as the prototype progresses.

The Value of Prototyping in Code

Even though there is an ever-growing list of different design tools, each with subtly different propositions and purposes when it comes to prototyping and creating usable interfaces, I can safely say that nothing is as flexible or as representative of a finished product than something written in code for the environment that it will ultimately be released into – whether that be the web or a native application for a specific operating system. That is not to say that those design tools do not have their place in the design process, or the larger software development life cycle, but that they can only deliver effectively in their areas of specialism.

For example, a tool like the InVision web app allows designers to link together a collection of screen designs created in a visual design tools such as Photoshop or Sketch, and it can even help the designer to create interactive elements with overlays, transitions, and other simple effects, but the results will lack the level of intricacy achievable with code.

Axure gives designers the ability to create interactive prototypes to create proof-of-concept prototypes, and it can enable the designer to produce something that can be used in a usability test setting. Again, the level of detail is lacking when compared to the possibilities that can be attained when building prototypes in code, but Axure provides a more advanced set of capabilities, such as adaptive layouts, and the ability to utilize JavaScript to create more detailed interactions with data and content.

Both of these tools (as well as the multitude of other prototyping applications) have their plus points in how and when a designer utilizes them within their design process. They are essentially a means to an end, a set of tools that allows the designer to progress their ideas in an iterative fashion, and discount the avenues that do not promise to fulfill the goals of both the user and the business.

These prototyping tools are useful in the day-to-day workflow of a designer who may be building out prototypes of features and user journeys within a product, but this level of efficiency comes at a cost. Firstly, the tools can be restrictive. In a lot of cases, especially in the early stages of the iterative design process, these tools have exactly what the designers need: the ability to create a proof of concept that is interactive enough to gain an understanding of the user's needs and frustrations.

As a lone designer within a small team, it can be very easy to hide behind the tools; to dive in to the creative process to produce a prototype, and only emerge at the other side with a fleshed out, testable prototype. You may have seen this for yourself within your own teams. We're all human beings, and not even the best designer in the world is

135

infallible when it comes to their design decisions, especially if they are working alone in a siloed environment. These situations are where you are able to aid the designer by lending them your skills.

Benefits of Collaborative Prototyping

Hand-coded prototypes have a rather specific place when it comes to prototyping. They can provide an experience as closes as possible to what it would be in a live, real-world situation. It fits well with the ability to conduct usability testing within the medium that the user will ultimately interact with it when live. Even though there are many ways to create shortcuts to place those software-generated prototypes in the environments where they will eventually go live in, they are still not as closely representative of the finished article.

There will be a wide variety of skill sets that can be found in designers when it comes to creating the highest fidelity prototypes. Some designers will be completely hands-off when it comes to code, and are not inclined to learn how to build something with code themselves. At the other end of the scale. you will have those who are more than proficient in building production quality websites and applications, although they may not be as familiar with cutting edge tooling and approaches to modern web and application development. In both of these scenarios, and everywhere in between, a developer will always have the chance to make a positive impact with the ability to impart their knowledge and skills, not only with regard to the project, but also to the designers.

At the upper end of the scale, with the designers that are more proficient coders, the benefits that a developer can provide will largely come from their deeper understanding of modern standards and techniques. You will be able to provide a level of knowledge of your own code base as well as the possibilities that exist and could be utilized, even if they are not yet implemented in your product. Personally, although I have been a web developer for the best part of two decades, my own focus has shifted to user experience design, meaning that my fundamental knowledge of how to build websites and applications remains, but my lack of day-to-day practice has meant that newer evolutions of standards, technologies, and frameworks are not as well understood as I would have expected them to be in the past.

Today, from my perspective as a designer, I will rely on the knowledge of the developers in my team to guide me in the areas that I am lacking a depth of knowledge that I would formerly be more accustomed to. Knowing what could be possible allows us to create more innovative prototypes to gauge the appetite of our users for new patterns and approaches to solving a given problem. By leaning on the skills and knowledge of the developers that I work with, together we can create interactive versions of the possible futures of our products and features.

Down at the other end of the scale, the positive effects that developers can have by lending their skills to the designers that are lacking in coding knowledge is far greater in comparison to those who have at least some experience coding. Here, the developer is the key to being able to deliver a high-fidelity prototype that can be used by the user experience designer in their usability testing. The key to this working well is collaboration. In Chapter 5 we looked at how we can improve the designer/developer relationship, and the collaboration required between the two disciplines in order to streamline the design and development workflows; prototyping is another window of opportunity to reinforce this understanding and gain the benefits earlier in the life cycle of a project.

With developers collaborating with designers in the prototyping stages of a product, the teams are able to avoid common pitfalls that can occur when you resort to a design handover; a knowledge gap in what is possible for the team to build, as well as a lack of understanding of the intentions behind the design and the decisions made that lead to the resulting interface and experience design. We should be more reliant on the members of our team rather than documentation and the tools we use. Building an understanding between these two disciplines has a compounding effect on the understanding between team members and contributes to a more efficient and effective product team.

Building a Valuable Prototype

The real value of prototypes built with code comes from the ability to provide users with the closest possible experience to a finished product. If we imagine that we are following the extreme prototyping methodology discussed earlier in this chapter, we can create what looks to be a fully functioning feature within an app, and only by utilizing front-end code without the integration of any back-end services.

As an example, we'll use a search function for narrowing down a list of customer accounts in within a hypothetical billing system. The functionality required in this particular interface is for the user to be able to enter a unique ID for a product in order to find the particular item the user is looking for. Figure 9-2 shows an example of what this screen could look like.

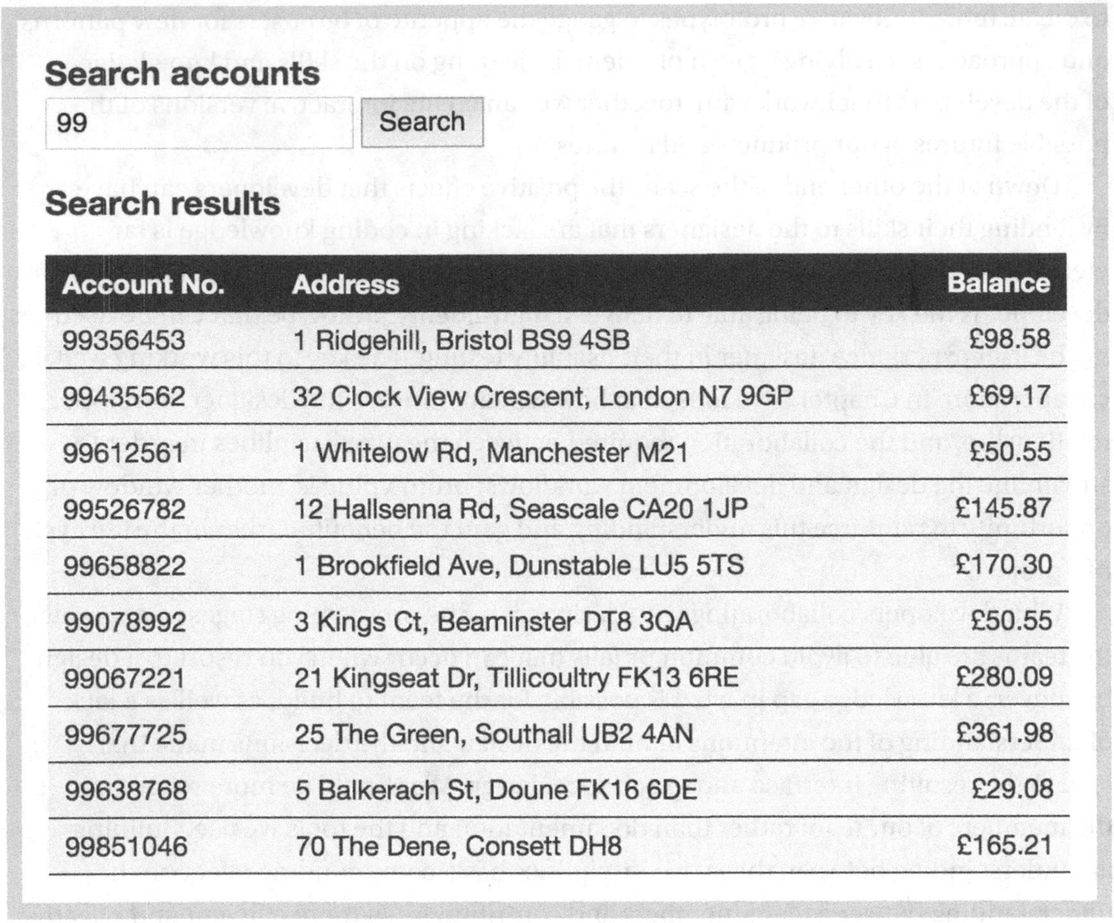

Search accounts

| 99 | | Search |

Search results

Account No.	Address	Balance
99356453	1 Ridgehill, Bristol BS9 4SB	£98.58
99435562	32 Clock View Crescent, London N7 9GP	£69.17
99612561	1 Whitelow Rd, Manchester M21	£50.55
99526782	12 Hallsenna Rd, Seascale CA20 1JP	£145.87
99658822	1 Brookfield Ave, Dunstable LU5 5TS	£170.30
99078992	3 Kings Ct, Beaminster DT8 3QA	£50.55
99067221	21 Kingseat Dr, Tillicoultry FK13 6RE	£280.09
99677725	25 The Green, Southall UB2 4AN	£361.98
99638768	5 Balkerach St, Doune FK16 6DE	£29.08
99851046	70 The Dene, Consett DH8	£165.21

Figure 9-2. *An example account list screen with a search form*

By entering something in the search form, we need to simulate the search function working as if it were interrogating a set of data and updating the interface accordingly. Without having to build a database or utilize an API, we can build a prototype that replicates the user experience without investing too much thought into the technological architecture that would be required to support such a feature in a live environment.

At this stage, we want to avoid thinking about the technical constraints at this stage; this limits the possibilities. With our priority being the delivery of a better experience to the user, we put ourselves in a better position to achieve this when we avoid the constraints of current systems. It opens the avenues for creative ways in which we can look to work around these constraints later in the software development life cycle in order to deliver that improved user experience.

In order to build something that behaves like a search function, without it really being one, we need to get a little creative. First, we'll need a form into which the user can enter their search criteria.

```
<form onsubmit="return false;">
        <label for="search">Search accounts</label>
        <input type="text" id="search">
        <input type="submit" id="searchbutton" Value="Search">
</form>
```

Let's assume we already have a full set of test data that we can use as an example within this static page, perhaps from an online generator, or maybe using a dump of real data from your organization's data store. We have then created each record as part of a data table in the HTML, which could look something like this:

```
<h2>Search results</h2>
<div id="results" style="display: none;">
  <table>
    <thead>
      <tr>
        <th>Account number</th>
        <th>Address</th>
        <th>Balance</th>
      </tr>
    </thead>
    <tbody>
      <tr>
        <td>99356453</td>
        <td>1 Ridgehill, Bristol BS9 4SB</td>
        <td>£98.58</td>
      </tr>
      <tr>
        <td>99435562</td>
        <td>32 Clock View Crescent, London N7 9GP</td>
        <td>£69.17</td>
      </tr>
```

```
        <tr>
            <td>99612561</td>
            <td>1 Whitelow Rd, Manchester M21</td>
            <td>£50.55</td>
        </tr>
    </tbody>
</table>
</div>
```

When a user comes to our search screen, we wouldn't want them to see hundreds of records straight away; that's not what we would expect in this hypothetical scenario, so we can hide them away with CSS. Each row in the table could would have some additional styling:

```
<tr style="display: none;">
  <td>99356453</td>
  <td>1 Ridgehill, Bristol BS9 4SB</td>
  <td>£98.58</td>
</tr>
```

Now, I know that inline CSS is a classic faux pas when it comes to modern web development, but we must bear in mind that we are building a prototype, as quickly as possible, without the concerns of best practice or milliseconds of performance becoming a factor.

Now we need to think about how we can display any of the table rows that match the input of the user in the search form. We could try to match content within the HTML, but that may take a fair bit of JavaScript development work in to achieve, so let's think of a way in which we could make a shortcut. If we were to add a data attribute to each row of the table, we could then use JavaScript to match the input of the form, and then display the rows that match the input. Here's what a row from that table would now look like in code:

```
<tr data-account="99356453" style="display: none;">
  <td>99356453</td>
  <td>1 Ridgehill, Bristol BS9 4SB</td>
  <td>£98.58</td>
</tr>
```

Now we need a bit of JavaScript to create the faux search function. In this case, we utilize the jQuery library, just because it will give us easy to access functions that can help us to achieve our goals for this particular prototype. Here's what that code for that function could look like.

```
<script>
  $("#searchbutton").on("click", function(){
    dosearch();
  });

  function dosearch(){
    $('#results tr').hide();
    var term = $("#search").val();
    var accountItems = $('tr[data-account*="' + term + '"]').length;
    if (accountItems > 0){
      $('tr[data-account*="' + term + '"]').show();
    }
  }
}
</script>
```

Although this works, it presents us with another kind of problem from the user's perspective; the search is perceived to be too quick to return the results, and therefore it is less believable to the user. The point at which the button to perform the search is clicked, there is a user expectation for there to be a delay while something happens in the background – a query to be run on a database to find what the user is looking for, for instance – before returning the results and displaying them. A delay between 0.2 and 1.0 seconds means that the user notices the delay, but it is quick enough for them not to lose their sense of "flow" while performing the task. In order to replicate that feeling of the system performing the search, we can add a delay to the display of results, along with a bit of feedback to the user.

First, we can add some more HTML to display while the search function appears to be running.

```
<h2>Search results</h2>
<div id="searching" style="display: none;">
  <p>Searching...</p>
</div>
<div id="results" style="display: none;">
```

141

Than we can utilize that new element to create a state of feedback for the user while the search seems to be happening in the background.

```
function dosearch(){

  if($("#results").filter(':hidden')){
    $("#results").hide();
    $("#searching").show();
    setTimeout(function() {
      $("#searching").hide();
      $("#results").show();
    }, 1000);
  }

  $('#results tr').hide();
```

And with that, we have a single, static HTML page that behaves like a real-world application with a dataset that can be easily searched. Without building an entire infrastructure to support this kind of functionality, we are now able to put this functioning interface in front of our users and run usability testing to uncover any flaws in our approach, gain insight into a user's expectation, and work toward a final solution. You can find a working example of this at https://codepen.io/uxfordevelopers/pen/VBOVWd.

Some would argue that this kind of work is distracting to a developer, that they should be focused on the delivery of features and products for release. While this may be the main reason developers are employed, the provision of time to explore, experiment, and learn should not be brushed aside. Prototyping in this way allows both designers and developers, the whole team in fact, to explore concepts and approaches that they would not necessarily be able to while working on a tight schedule for delivery. There is fun to be had in this type of work, exercising the brain to come up with ways in which to replicate a real-world implementation by ultimately tricking the user into thinking it is something that really works.

Others may argue that this is not as beneficial to the development team than it would be to creating the products or features themselves. To be rather blunt, that is an extremely blinkered view of what it means to be part of a development team, as well as a product team. To only concentrate on the delivery, and to be measured by your performance in that aspect alone, is to ignore the benefits that the rest of the product team have to offer, not to developers, but to the product and its users. Working together with designers, business analysts, and product owners shows you how much of an impact you can have on the user experience that comes from this wider perspective of fulfilling the needs of our users.

Evaluation with Usability Testing

Throughout this chapter, we have mentioned usability testing a great deal, but you may not be fully aware of what this entails, and how it differs from the kind of testing that developers are more familiar with in the software development life cycle.

Rather than using automated test scripts and internal testing teams to uncover bugs against a set of predefined requirements, usability testing focuses on the user being able to complete their tasks, and can be measured against the five quality components established by Jakob Nielsen of the Nielsen Norman Group.

- Learnability: How easy is it for users to accomplish basic tasks the first time they encounter the design?

- Efficiency: Once users have learned the design, how quickly can they perform tasks?

- Memorability: When users return to the design after a period of not using it, how easily can they re-establish proficiency?

- Errors: How many errors do users make, how severe are these errors, and how easily can they recover from the errors?

- Satisfaction: How pleasant is it to use the design?

A user will be placed in a room with your product and asked to carry out a number of tasks, while being asked to think out loud throughout so we can understand their thought processes and why they make the decisions they make. The tasks we ask the user to undertake helps us to reach the answer to the question: Does it do what users need?

This is the crux of the matter. Everything we do as developers affects the user experience. We can build the fastest loading interface, feedback mechanisms that build trust with the user, and deliver a top-quality product with a vast array of potentially useful features.

But all of that is for nothing if the product does not do what the user needs.

This is why usability testing is so important; it guides us on what we need to create to cater to the needs of our users. We do not gain insights into how people actually use our products from automated scripts and functional testing. A successful test in standard development terms proves that a piece of code or functionality works as it is intended, whereas a successful usability test can prove or disprove our hypotheses around a user's behavior and how they *expect* the product to function.

Why Usability Testing Is Important

The common types of testing carried out in software projects focuses on the code, how it functions, and whether it conforms to the specification against which it was written. Even User Acceptance Testing (UAT) can often be performed by testers employed by the organization rather than with – as the title would suggest – actual users. The perspective of those outside of our product team, and outside of the organization, provide a hugely undervalued perspective on how our product should function in order to serve them better. If we exclude the user, we are simply using our best guess to create a product that we believe our users will make use of. In today's world, with access to unprecedented amounts of data about our users, and access to real people who use our products, taking our best guess is simply not good enough to be able to compete with our organization's competitors in the digital space.

It does not take a huge amount of research in order to gain the insights need to move your product forward in terms of usability. Nielsen Norman Group recommends that you test with five users when conducting a usability study. This conclusion is drawn from two main influencing factors: return on investment for the business and diminishing returns on usability findings. With regard to return on investment, the more participants we have to recruit in order to conduct a usability testing session, the greater the cost of running a set of those sessions becomes. On average, testing a prototype with five people helps you to uncover almost as many usability problems as you would if you doubled, or even tripled, the number of participants. The combination of the diminishing returns and the return on investment create a strong case for only testing with five users for a single set of hypotheses that you may be looking to prove (or disprove).

Even testing with just one user will uncover obvious usability problems that may have otherwise slipped under the radar, completely unnoticed, and ending up in the release of your feature or product. This is not just something aimed at developers, designers, but the product team as a whole, as well as the stakeholders; everyone involved in the project is an expert to some degree in the product you are delivering. This means that your level of understanding has been acquired over the time that you have worked on the project, and this is a level of knowledge that your users are very unlikely to possess. This curse of knowledge, believe it or not, can actually become a positive force for the improvement of your product; it helps to establish trust with your stakeholders that you are creating solutions that are the most relevant to your users, that you are constantly evaluating your work and refocusing where required in order to build the right thing. This is far more valuable to any stakeholder worth their salt than listening only to internal opinions from which the direction of design and development is taken for your product.

The findings from usability testing sessions can help to justify your approaches, they can help to refine your requirements, and they can be used to clarify internal expectations around the product you are looking to deliver. You may start out with a vision for a particular feature or product as a whole, but as you work through the proposition and begin to put your work in front of real people who would hopefully become your future users, you can greatly reduce possible risks to the business associated with the product, and in turn reduce the costs of redevelopment and maintenance before the product arrives at a point where these would be required. In short, usability testing prevents additional work and guides you down the right path when building digital products for people to use.

What Constitutes a Successful Usability Test?

As we have mentioned before, a successful usability test is measured in a different way to a successful test with regard to functionality or code. The success of a usability test can be measured by what we learn about both our users and our product, not down to the level of detail of the code passing a set of unit tests. A successful test is not necessarily one where the user completes a task in the way we thought they would, or indeed the way we wanted them to. The success of a usability test is measured in the outcomes. It is in the validation of our hypotheses, and the invalidation of them. Oftentimes, a failed hypothesis has more benefit than a successful one.

Imagine, for example, we have a navigation component that lives in the left-hand column on a web application dashboard. This navigation contains all of the elements for traversing through the various features of the product, as well as links to the dashboard and managing user preferences. We can form a hypothesis that the user preferences could be removed from this navigation, separated out, and moved to a more commonly found location as per other well-used web applications, toward the top-right corner of the screen. We can hypothesize that users will be able to discover the link that will allow them to update their preferences more efficiently than when compared to the same option placed alongside all of the other navigation options within the product.

Figure 9-3 shows a wireframe of a web application consisting of very little detail, with only shapes to represent elements on the page such as links in the left-hand navigation, a table of content in the main part of the screen, and a header bar that houses the new link to the user preference in the top-right corner.

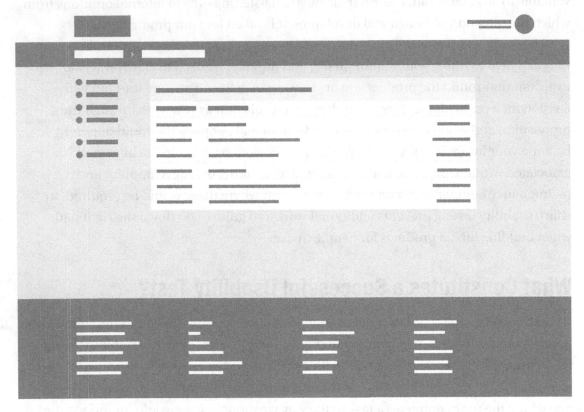

Figure 9-3. *Example of wireframes testing the scenario above*

Despite the lack of details, it is possible to set a task for the user asking where they would expect to find the functionality to change any of their personal preferences for the application. This provides us with an insight into where a user would expect to find this functionality based on their knowledge of websites and applications in general, and that they expect your website or application to work in the same ways as the others they use.

Alternatively, you can test users with a higher-fidelity set of designs, portraying the different options for layout. This can be measured simply by the time it takes the user to find the function they require in the interfaces presented to them in the test. We can make comparisons against the currently existing interface by running the same test and comparing the results, but we have to be careful of skewing the data. The order of these two tests must be taken into consideration, as whichever of the interfaces is shown first can have a negative impact on time for finding the same piece of functionality in the second interface, simply as the user has just discovered where to find it in the previous interface. You can look to negate this kind of bias in your results by changing the order in which these two interfaces are tested, or even look to only test one of the designs with a single user, but testing them both the same number of times across a number of participants.

Other hypotheses may be more detailed and nuanced, and require the testing of an entire user journey from beginning to end. Although the hypothesis being tested in this kind of scenario could essentially be measured in the user's ability to complete the journey successfully of not, the real value comes from the user's thought process throughout. In most usability testing scenarios, the user will be continually encouraged to "think out loud," and commentate on what they're thinking as they attempt to work through a journey in order to complete the task they are given as part of the test. In these usability testing scenarios, the value is in this commentary, in what the user is thinking, why they are thinking that, and what they think they should be doing next. Regardless of whether the user actually completes the task or not is nowhere near as informative as the insights they give us into their thought processes as they work their way through the task.

This is a good example of outcomes outweighing the output. What we learn from these kinds of usability testing sessions, the outcomes that give us insight into the way users think and behave, have a far greater impact on our future work than just being able to prove that our journeys and functionality enable the user to complete a task. The percentage of users that complete a journey successfully can be a useful metric, but discovering that users don't want to complete that particular journey in the manner prescribed by the design of the product; that there are better ways to tackle a particular problem that users have experienced elsewhere and found less problems with; or how they felt when reading the words around the components they were interacting with and whether they understood them; these are just some examples of outcomes that don't go into making a graph that goes up and to the right to just make stakeholders happy. This is the fuel to stoke the fire of improving the lives of your users, of real people.

Summary

In this chapter we have taken a look at the iterative design process, and how this lends itself to more modern approaches to digital product design in the form of minimum viable products, prototyping, and continuous evaluation of these. We examined what makes an MVP valuable to our users, what happens when they are not, and how the user experience can benefit from using an MVP approach to design.

We looked at both low- and high-fidelity prototyping and how developers can have a significant input on high-fidelity prototyping, and the four prototyping models that would benefit from a developer's input. We went in-depth as to why there is value in prototyping in code, the wider benefits of doing this collaboratively with designers, and how sharing your knowledge can benefit the other members of the team in understanding what can be possible.

By using an example of a prototype, we looked at why throw-away code still has value, even if it is not in the reusability of the code itself, but in the value that it provides in understanding our users and how that can shape the future of our products.

Finally, we looked at how we can evaluate our prototypes with usability testing, what that involves, and how successful user tests aren't just about a user being able to complete a journey or a task, but the value and insight we gain from how they go about the completion of that task.

The utilization of the iterative design process and the use of prototyping in conjunction with usability testing help us to gain insight into what users need and expect without going to the lengths of building fully fledged products, without doing a large amount of development work just to find that what we have built is of no use to our users. This process will save developers from wasted work, while giving you the insight as to why you are building these products, and who you are building them for.

CHAPTER 10

The Path Ahead

The purpose of this book was not for you to become an expert in user experience, or even in one of the specific disciplines within the wider sphere of user experience, but to increase your awareness of the people who use the things that you build, to understand the importance of the user experience, and how you can adapt the way you work to focus on your users.

Through the course of reading this book, we have covered the definition of user experience as it pertains to the perspective of the developer, and its importance to the software that you build. We have spent time looking at how we can change our perspective to understand how the work we do impacts the experience of the users of our software, how we can empathize with our users, and train the focus of our work to benefit them. These fundamentals – core to the understanding of user experience, and how we go about the work we do through an iterative design process – give us an understanding as to the why and how of what goes into designing and developing a better user experience.

The fact that you have read about all of the aspects of user experience mentioned throughout this book already puts you way ahead of other developers; those who have neglected to explore what user experience entails have less to offer than you now do. Even if you do not start to implement the things you have learned in the course of reading this book, you are already endowed with the knowledge that will make it far easier for designers to work with you and vice versa.

All we have really covered in this book are the fundamentals of user experience, with an added perspective of how this vast field can benefit developers today. The depth into which you can delve into any of the different disciplines within the wider encompassing sphere of user experience is remarkable, but again, the purpose of this book is not for you to become an expert in user experience.

Then there are the underlying foundations in both software development and user experience. For the former, there are best practices that should be adhered to within the languages in which you code, accessibility principles, and other methodologies that lend

© Westley Knight 2019
W. Knight, *UX for Developers*, https://doi.org/10.1007/978-1-4842-4227-8_10

structure to the software development process. The latter is underpinned by the use of user research within a large and flexible framework of tools and techniques.

Even though there is so much room to grow your understanding in either development or user experience as individual fields, my experience has shown that a combination of both proves more valuable to your teams, as well as to you as an individual and the work you do.

The value in what you choose to learn lies in the ability for you to then apply your newly acquired knowledge. Is your organization switching to a new technology stack? If so, you should prioritize your learning of the new languages or frameworks that you will be employing. As you do so, the principles and best practices that you follow at a higher level (not those associated with a particular language or framework) will still apply to your work. The same is true of the underlying principles of user experience.

There is never a single black and white answer as to how to best approach the work you do. Your given priorities and where you intend to place you focus will shift on a continuous basis, but those underlying foundations are what you build upon; they are the compass that will help to guide you on your journey of learning throughout your career. Whatever your particular situation, your understanding of user experience that you have gained from this book provides you with another pillar that will support what you do toward the betterment of the products that you get to work on.

The Next Evolution of the Developer

Your skills as a developer do not start and end with your ability to write code and deliver to a functional specification. In order to stay relevant and valuable, you must become aware of how your work impacts on the other members of your team, and the people who interact with the software that you build. Simply knowing your framework of choice inside out makes you a good technical developer, but that value barely reaches beyond the boundaries of the developers that your work with. A truly valuable developer is one who can deliver value for their colleagues and their users through their technical knowledge, their skill in writing code, and their ability to place the user at the heart of all of the decisions they make.

The next evolution of successful developers considers far more than the technical constraints, the functional specification, and what is possible with newly emerging technologies. They will understand the impact of their work on the lives of real human beings, of the people whose lives will be made a little easier by the work that they do.

To be part of that evolution of developers, user experience is a lynchpin upon which your future may depend. Without a care for the eventual experience that you create, you will simply be seen as a tool of implementation, called upon when required for a particular job, and put to one side until that need arises again. To be a staple of the whole software development life cycle, of both design and development, your consideration of the user experience is not just recommended, but it is of paramount importance. It is the competitive edge that all organizations crave in order for their digital products to become a real success, and that means allowing more than just the designers to care about and have an input into creating a better user experience.

The Collaborating Developer

Beyond that understanding of the user experience, the ability to collaborate with other disciplines within your team is key to your ongoing success. The future of both development and user experience design lies in greater collaboration between these two disciplines.

It's probably fair to say that a developer learning from other developers will make them a better developer, technically speaking. But this approach alone will leave you lacking in the flexibility to adapt, and even leave you languishing at the bottom of the list when it comes to having a say in the direction that the products you work on are going. Developers learning from designers, designers learning from developers, and the wider team learning from your knowledge, your skills, and the way in which you collaborate, make you more valuable to the team and give you a broader range of experience upon which to draw when making your decisions.

But developers learning from users is the most important of all. By focusing on the user; by understanding the way they think and behave; building your empathy with them; and working with your team in prototyping, usability testing, and even design and research, you will gain the insight you once never knew you needed to. This will give you the biggest advantage when it comes to your value to the team, to your organizations, and will ultimately show in the products you deliver to the user. By getting to know your users by discovering how they think, how they act, and the why that drives them, you can become a voice for your users within your organization. You will become one of the internal representatives of your users, bridging the gap that will allow others to understand who they are designing and building their products for. This is not something that only those who have "UX" in their job title should be concerned about nurturing. Although this understanding may sit firmly within their wheelhouse, when an entire product team understands their users, they all become evangelists for the improvement of the user experience.

The Strategic Developer

Before reading this book, had you ever thought about how the things you build affect the lives of the people that use them? I mean, really thought about it? Is there a particular thing that you were really proud of creating as you knew it would really make the difference to someone using your piece of software? Perhaps you can think back and find something that you could have thought of in this way, but didn't at the time? It's not a bad thing if you didn't, it's simply a reflection of how you were working at the time. I had spent many years only focusing on the work in front of me, it's immediate impact on the people closest to me in a professional sense, my colleagues in my team, whether that was at an agency or in-house. I had what is referred to as a more "tactical" view of the work I was doing, rather than a more "strategic" perspective.

On so many levels, I would be working to a much shorter time frame, within a shorter field of view. The realization that the work you do lasts for much longer than you may have thought, and that it may have far more reach, and impact on far more people, suddenly opens up a whole world of new concerns and thoughts about how to handle the way you work; to give you a more strategic view.

Imagine you are building a small component for a website, a newsletter sign-up form, for example. From a tactical perspective, you are looking at how to build this small form component: considering the semantics to use and the functionality around what should happen when the form is submitted. You are concerned about the component itself, and that it works as intended. Take a metaphorical step back from that individual component and consider the wider picture. This newsletter sign-up form is part of a much larger ecosystem of numerous other components, all of which will appear in different areas around the website, and may need to be presented differently in conjunction with other elements, or even change their functionality. When you have a view of this critical information, you begin to consider the consequences of dropping your new component into environments that hadn't been considered previously, and how you can work on your component to successfully integrate with every other component it will find itself appearing alongside.

You become aware that this component you have been working on is just one small piece in a much larger puzzle. The detail within that small piece is still of importance, but it must be able to fit with many other small pieces to make a functional and usable whole. By thinking more strategically, by considering the impact that the work you are doing – even in small component pieces as per the example above – you can factor in the wider implications of your choices.

Take the widely publicized failure of the Healthcare.gov website on its launch in October 2013, for example. From the difficult, sometimes seemingly impossible task of users simply attempting to sign up was compounded by messages of "please wait" and "Sorry, we can't find that page" throughout the website. This website was a huge undertaking, worked on by at least two teams, apparently working in complete isolation from each other, tasked with integrating over 100 different computer systems across the United States. Without these teams taking a step back from their own work, to take stock and to consider the whole, to work together toward a common goal, the resulting system was almost completely unusable. Even if you never work on a project of this scale, the same applies for everything you work on; this all matters to the end user, so be sure to remember that.

So why not take a step back from the product or feature you are building, and think about why you are building it. Who is it for? Why are you building it for them? Centering this strategic thinking around your users helps you to concentrate on the right problems for you to be solving, the ones that have a bigger positive impact on the user, guiding you away from undertaking unnecessary work. Being able to switch between the view from ten thousand feet and the detail of what's right in front of you in the code editor is a hugely beneficial skill that can be nurtured over time, allowing you to constantly evaluate the work you are doing, and whether it fits with the strategic aim; whether it will work for your users.

The User Experience Developer

The constant advancement in technology is responsible for a number of job titles appearing in the world of digital that did not exist a decade or so ago: iOS Developer, Android Developer, UX Designer. And yet, as technology evolves, so does the expertise of those who utilize it, who find new ways of innovating, giving rise to the needs of different skills and abilities in different roles. Over the past few years I've seen a number of tweets, blog posts, and articles on a job title of "UX Developer." There are obviously mixed opinions on this job title appearing, some saying it is misleading or even go to the lengths of saying that it is sullying the name of those who do "real user experience work." I've even had the (mis)fortune to have been given the title "Senior UX/UI Developer" at one point in my career, simply as I was the senior front-end developer who wanted to utilize user research, prototyping, usability testing, along with a whole host of other skills that would usually be in the camp of a UX Designer. It was the best we could come up with to describe what it was that I did. But this is not necessarily what I want you, as a developer, to evolve into. I have mentioned many times throughout this book that it is not my intention to convert you into a UX Designer, Researcher, or whatever new roles may appear in the field of user experience in future.

However, there is a way in which you can be a user experience developer. Not in the way that you write code, or how you interpret findings from usability testing, but in how you can spread the word about user experience. Even with an understanding of only the fundamental aspects of user experience design that you have taken from within these pages, you can begin to foster a better understanding of what it takes to create better user experiences throughout your team and your organization. If that feels too daunting of a task for you, you can do the simplest of tasks, which is to support the UX designers and researchers in your team.

When in meetings with other developers, you will no doubt have conversations where someone will be rather disparaging to the work of a designer within their team. Perhaps they didn't consider a particular technical constraint, or a discussion boiled over about a particular aspect of what has been developed, which didn't reflect the designer's intention. Whatever it may be, you have the opportunity to help educate your fellow developer on what they may have been trying to achieve. That their focus is to deliver a better experience to the user, and really, that is what the developers should also be trying to do. Be there to facilitate discussion between warring parties, to help both sides understand where each of them is coming from, and why it is so important to do more work so that our users don't have to.

Breaking Your Old Habits

Not much of what you have learned from the previous chapters in this book will be instantly integrated into your day-to-day workflow without much thought. Much of the conceptual thinking, the psychology underpinning the decisions we make during the software development life cycle, will slowly seep into the way your work, but only if you make a sustained effort to consider this new plethora of input that helps to guide your decision making. Much like the syntax you learn for a specific programming language, the more you use it, the easier it is to recall. Over time, the way you apply what you have learned over and over, by adjusting your new approaches to new scenarios and recurring situations, this constant application becomes part of the way that you work.

Part of forming new habits will involve breaking some of your old habits. Question yourself and the way you work on whatever project you may be involved with right now. Is what you're doing right now going to benefit the user? Have the recent decisions you have made going to have a positive impact on the resulting experience? If not, ask yourself why. What questions did you neglect to ask before you made that decision? What would you have done differently had you asked that question before committing to your chosen course of action? You may not be able to go back and change your decisions, but you can learn from those past decisions to help you make better, more educated, user-focused choices moving forward.

You'll see the value in from this effort increase incrementally, over time. It will surface in how your collaboration with designers and other members of the team becomes more fluid, how your opinion on areas outside of development becomes more valued, and how your new focus on your users helps to build more successful and usable products.

Your habits may be very difficult to change, but you are in control of your attitude toward your work. As we discussed in Chapter 4, this kind of decision is within your sphere of control, and as such, you can make direct and impactful decisions about how you intend to approach your work in the future. Once you have mastered that change in your own outlook, your circle of influence becomes an area in which you can persuade others to begin thinking in a user-focused manner. You can begin to question whether the motivations of others are driven by user needs, and when any resistance is encountered, you can point to the ways in which you have changed your ways of thinking to show that it is both possible and beneficial to your collective work.

Brace for Change

You will no doubt face resistance within the hierarchy of your development team as you begin to place more emphasis on the user in your working practice. This is a very natural response as to this kind of change to the focus of your work. By aiming to deliver a better experience with your user firmly in mind rather than looking to deliver code that passes automated tests, delivers to functional specifications, and is completed in time to hit those release windows, you will bring the real benefits of your work to real people who will use your product.

There is a possibility that this shift in your focus may put you in a difficult position – particularly across the development team as a whole – arguing a case for users when your responsibility may have been purely focused on delivery to a set of requirements. In many organizations it is still true that as long as you develop to those requirements set out earlier in the software development life cycle, and that you have ticked all of the relevant boxes along the way, you have successfully met your criteria, you have done your job. To change the perception of what is required from a developer is, again, not something that will happen overnight, and it will take effort and steadfastness, but it will carry more gravitas when it is the developer themselves suggesting that they take more responsibility for the resulting user experience.

It is also a possibility that other disciplines may have an adverse reaction to developers educating themselves in relevant areas, outside of their core discipline, such as user experience. Putting to one side the fact that this may be reflective of a far-from-ideal working environment, what you bring to the table with this additional knowledge is more beneficial than may be first thought, and definitely does not have to figuratively step on anyone's toes. Even with a developer becoming involved in the earlier design phase of a project, this can help designers and business analysts to understand both the technical constraints and the numerous possibilities that could be leveraged from newer technologies and approaches. In less mature environments, this type of knowledge is both crucial and can be very much undervalued, and it is something that developers must strive to impart to their team to avoid making more costly mistakes later in the day.

You are able to help develop the understanding of user experience throughout your own team, to your developer colleagues across other teams, and even throughout the business. Best of all, you won't be alone in doing this, and you won't have to be front and center; you simply have to be there to support those working on the user experience, to back them up when needed, and to be a voice for the user within your organization. Remember that those who work in user experience – or those that simply have an appreciation for the user experience – will be the rocks upon which you can rely for support; they'll be there to answer your questions and help you on your journey.

Keeping Pace with Technology

We are all very aware of the rapid pace at which the world of technology moves forward, and with it, how much opportunity it brings to learn new programming languages, approaches, methodologies, and frameworks. This rapid advancement and seemingly endless opportunities also take a toll on us as individuals, and we can feel like we are being left behind, and that we must constantly be learning the latest and greatest things in order to stay relevant. Although these pressures may be ones that you place upon yourself, or are placed upon you by the organization you work for, if you view them in the same way that a business would when making decisions on where to invest their time and money, you can make the right decision based on the return on investment you we receive.

Although the rapid pace of this evolution from a technological standpoint is far beyond anything we may have experienced before, it does not, and nor should it, dictate the paths that you take in delivering your software to your users.

Alternatively, by a slower, more-considered evolution of your digital products, you will reduce the probable risks compared to switching to the latest JavaScript framework every time the next hottest thing is released. Utilizing a tried and trusted technology stack provides a robust and reliable foundation upon which you can look to introduce more modern approaches over time. This helps to manage changes to the user experience by only introducing new features in a drip-fed manner, only creating changes to existing experiences one piece at a time, minimizing the risk of alienating your users with a grand shift to a brand-new design that works in a completely different manner as to what existed before. There are examples of these kinds of broad changes to digital products and the negative impacts they can have. When Marks & Spencer in the United Kingdom redesigned and re-platformed their entire website, there were an astonishing number of problems ranging from people being unable to access their order history, to being completely unable to log in to their accounts. The success stories of the slowly evolving digital products that consider their users' needs, make informed decisions, and avoid big impact changes, don't make the headlines. The products keep working, they slowly evolving, and keep their user happy.

This is not to say that the implementation of a new framework would always result in a negative impact on the user experience, especially when handled well. Switching to newer technologies in a measured and considered way can also result in big benefits for the end user, as well as the developers who continue to work on improving the product.

The key to keeping up with emerging technologies is to only entertain and educate yourself with those that will contribute to your ability to create a better user experience, while trying to avoid being swept up in the sales patter and social media circus that may surround the next big thing.

Get Comfortable with the Idea of Making Design Decisions

Anyone who influences the outcome of a design is making design decisions...

—Jared Spool

Back in Chapter 4 we discussed how developers make design decisions every time they sit down to implement a component or product feature of some kind. Regardless of whether or not any individual in any discipline within your team has any education when it comes to design, everyone still makes design decisions. These decisions can be both direct and indirect. Indirect design decisions tend to happen earlier in the software developer life cycle, and even before it has begun in some cases. Direct design decisions take place nearer the point of implementation, with decisions impacting the user experience hopefully having some grounding in research as to what benefits the user. Either way, all of these design decisions can be made by anyone at any time, regardless of their experience with, or understanding of, the impact their decision may have on the resulting user experience.

But the line where design starts and stops is an extremely blurry one, and the point at which design ends and implementation begins can be very different from the perception of whomsoever is asking that particular question. Rather than arguing as there the line resides, better communication and collaboration between the disciplines in your team will transcend these boundaries, and allow clear decision making and thoughtful choices to be made for the benefit of the user.

From what you have learned from this book, you are now able to consider the user when making decisions during your day-to-day work; you are able to make more informed decisions. You have the ability to now ask "Why?" when it comes to any decisions that have been made by other members of your team or organization, and to evaluate how much benefit it drives for the user. You must also remember to apply this questioning to your own decisions as you make them throughout your day. Remember that you have to be a representative of the user in their absence, that the work you do will ultimately benefit them and provide them with a better experience.

By validating your day-to-day decisions, design related or otherwise, against the yardstick of creating a better user experience, you will become comfortable in making these design decisions without having to change your job title to "Designer," as will your colleagues from other disciplines as well as your own.

Creating Enduring Change

You do not need to be a master of user experience to be able to have a positive impact upon it that will be of benefit to your users. You do not need 10 thousand hours practicing with the tools, techniques, and approaches utilized by the different disciplines within the sphere of user experience to be able to share what you have learned. I have only been a UX Designer since transitioning from my role as a developer five years ago, and yet here I am, writing this book to share what I have learned, what I now understand, from a perspective that I hope other developers will be able to appreciate and perhaps relate to.

You now know enough to facilitate discussions around user experience. You know enough to feel empowered to speak up on behalf of the user when others may not. You have a deeper understanding of the work that the user experience designers and researchers in your organization carry out, and you can offer support to them in any capacity in which you feel comfortable. You also offer a different perspective: a technical perspective that means you probably know more of what is possible than the designers. You are able to provide better solutions that design may not have even considered because they don't have that technical background. The key thing is to offer up your knowledge and your assistance to others consistently, to always have the user in mind when working with others, and to help further their understanding and the importance of the user experience.

Fostering change for the betterment of the user experience is not something that will happen overnight, but will need your support in the things that you can provide support with, on an ongoing basis. This is the way in which cultural change in an organization will take hold, and developers can go some way to help the advancement of this understanding, this appreciation for the needs of the user, and their experience with your products.

In Conclusion

In this final chapter, we have covered what you are now able to do with the skills you have learned throughout this book: how you are able to support your colleagues who work in user experience fields and share the knowledge you have gained to your fellow developers.

How far you want to take your new understanding of user experience and how it will benefit you as a developer is completely up to you. Maybe it's enough for you just to be aware, and that's completely okay. The fact that you have an awareness of the work that is put into the design process to make a better experience for the user gives you the perspective needed to help facilitate this without having to dive deep into the theory and start becoming an integral part of the design process. Alternatively, you can get really hands on, open yourself up to a whole new world of user experience that will help you to become a more valuable member of the team, and another voice for the user representing their needs.

Index

A

Accessibility issues, 26
Adobe XD, 130
Agile methodologies, 7
Animation
    affordance, 122
    CSS and JavaScript, 121
    delight, 125–126
    digital product, 121
    feedback, 123–124
    focus, 123
    guidance of developers, 121
    orientation, 124–125
    software development life cycle, 121
    user interface, 121
Automatic gearbox, 75–76
Avoidance of unnecessary elements, 74–75

B

Back-end developer, 38
Bleeding-edge technology, 1
Business objectives
    designing and building product, 30
    digital technology, 32
    digital user experience and sustainable
        product, 30
    Google Analytics, 31
    knowledge, skills, and tools, 32
    KPIs and OKRs, 31
    metrics, 31
    SMART goals, 32–33
    strategic decision, 30
    user-centered approach, 32
    user-centered design, 30–31
Business perspective, 14

C

Card design pattern
    BBC website, 81
    Pinterest, 80
    Rightmove, 80
    wireframe version, 81
Card sorting, 86
Changing gear, 75–76
CHAOS Report, 23
Cognitive biases, 66
Cognitive load
    Hick's Law, 69–70
    Miller's Number, 69
    working memory, 68
Collaborating developer, 151–152
Communication
    analytical and logical approach, 61
    barriers, 59–60
    clarity, 57
    criticism, 55
    curse of knowledge, 62
    designer/developer relationships, 58–59
    developer role, 51

© Westley Knight 2019
W. Knight, *UX for Developers*, https://doi.org/10.1007/978-1-4842-4227-8

Printed in the United States
By Bookmasters

Printed in the United States
By Bookmasters